Striving to promote and implement the preservation and conservation of the historic monuments and cultural heritage of the Deccan within a holistic environment and social context

Deccan Heritage Foundation Ltd
Suite 1, 3rd Floor, 11-12 St James's
Square, London SW1Y 4LB, UK

Deccan Heritage Foundation India
12, First Floor, Temple Trees Row,
Cauvery Colony, Near Koramangala, 1st Block,
Bangalore 560047
admin@deccan-heritage-foundation.org

www.deccan-heritage-foundation.org

DESIGN Nidhi Sah
PRINTING JAK Printers Pvt Ltd

ISBN 978-93-89305-10-4

Second Jaico Impression 2023

PUBLISHED BY
Jaico Publishing House
A-2 Jash Chambers,
7-A Sir Phirozshah Mehta Road
Fort, Mumbai - 400 001
jaicopub@jaicobooks.com
www.jaicobooks.com

THE HOYSALA LEGACY
BELUR, HALEBIDU, SOMANATHAPURA

The Deccan Heritage Foundation would like to acknowledge the endowment of **Marcello and Sandra Cattaneo Adorno** and participation of **Giacomo and Emanuela Cattaneo Adorno**. This publication is dedicated to the memory of their mother, the **Marchesa Carlotta Cattaneo Adorno**.

THE HOYSALA LEGACY
BELUR, HALEBIDU, SOMANATHAPURA

KAMALIKA BOSE AND GEORGE MICHELL

PHOTOGRAPHY Surendra Kumar

CONTENTS

PREVIOUS PAGES

PAGE 1
Belur, Chennakeshava Temple, entrance *gopura* and *dhvajastambha*

PAGE 3
Somanathapura, Keshava Temple, dancing Vishnu on the north tower

PAGES 4 AND 5 (TITLE)
Belur, Chennakeshava Temple, maiden bracket figures on the *mandapa* exterior

PAGES 6 AND 7 (CONTENTS)
Somanathapura, Keshava Temple, basement friezes of elephants, horse-riders, *makaras* and *hamsas*

RIGHT
Belur, Chennakeshava Temple, Mohini figure on a *mandapa* column

PREFACE

Supreme monarchs of the southern Deccan from the late 11th century to the early 14th century, the Hoysala kings and queens, together with their ministers and commanders, all commissioned splendid Hindu and Jain monuments. Of these, none are finer than the temples at Belur, Halebidu and Somanathapura described in this guidebook. Each represents an outstanding aspect of Hoysala art. The Chennakeshava temple at Belur is celebrated for its brackets fashioned as alluring maidens, perhaps the most beautiful in all Indian sculpture. The Hoysaleshvara temple at Halebidu is cloaked with carvings of celestials portraying almost the entire spectrum of Hindu myth and legend. While the early 12th-century monuments at Belur and Halebidu signal the beginnings of the Hoysala achievement, the Keshava temple at Somanathapura, built some 150 years later, is an architectural jewel summing up the overall contribution of the Hoysalas. Both Belur and Halebidu are included in the "Sacred Ensemble of the Hoysalas", now on the tentative list of UNESCO's prestigious World Heritage Sites.

This guidebook has been written for visitors who wish to explore the three temple complexes in detail. Its introduction covers the historical background to the monuments, the role of patrons and artists, the different architectural styles perfected by Hoysala builders, and the themes visualised by the sculptors, many of who signed their work. The following descriptions of the temples are intended to help visitors understand the complicated layouts and elevations of the buildings, and to direct their attention to the finest basement friezes, wall panels and doorway pediments, as well as the sculpted icons and ceiling panels of the interiors.

In the preparation of this volume, the authors have benefitted from helpful advice by Sandhya Harendra, Henry Noltie and Saarthak Singh. Srikara Dattatreya made welcome suggestions and also contributed summaries of the main narratives depicted in the sculptural friezes. R. Rajesh of Tours (S) India expertly managed our travels. As in previous Deccan Heritage Foundation guidebooks, Surendra Kumar has provided the splendid photographs that appear on almost every page.

Kamalika Bose and George Michell

Belur, Chennakeshava Temple, *mandapa* screen panel depicting a Hoysala king, probably Ballala II, with ministers, queen and retinue

INTRODUCTION

THE HOYSALAS

An abundance of inscriptions engraved onto stone slabs and copper plates, mostly in Old Kannada language and script, sheds light on the history of the Hoysalas, from their rise to power towards the end of the 11th century up until their demise in the middle of the 14th century. Originating in the forested hills of the Western Ghats, the Hoysalas began their careers in Angadi, a small town in southwestern Karnataka. From here they shifted to the important trade-route city of Belur, and then to Halebidu, to govern over much of the southern Deccan for more than 200 years. Theirs was a fertile domain through which flowed the Yagachi, Hemavati and Kaveri rivers. Together with dependable monsoon rains, these rivers made cattle grazing and cultivation of cereals possible, on which the kingdom's agrarian economy relied. (The present-day coffee and tobacco plantations were unknown in Hoysala times.) This affluence was supplemented by taxes on spinning, weaving, oil extracting, and preparation of sugar and jaggery. Commerce with the Arabian Sea ports beyond the Western Ghats led to imports of horses, pearls and other luxury goods in exchange for rich woods, precious stones, spices and medicinal plants. Profitable trade routes wended their way to the Tungabhadra valley region to the north, and beyond, into the territories of the Yadavas in Maharashtra. Other routes followed the course of the Kaveri to the southeast into Tamil Nadu, giving access to the prosperous territories of the Cholas and Pandyas. It was along these that the Hoysalas extended their sway, until their kingdom stretched for more than 500 kilometres from north to south, encompassing most of Karnataka. The considerable wealth amassed by the Hoysalas and their subordinates financed the construction of hundreds of temples during the 12th and 13th centuries, as well as numerous religious institutions like *mathas* and *agraharas*. This prosperity, however, led ultimately to disaster, attracting the attention of the invading Delhi troops who arrived in the northern Deccan in 1296, and in the following years proceeded southwards to pillage the Hoysala capital.

Before emerging as an independent lineage, the Hoysalas were subordinates of the Chalukya rulers based at Kalyana in northern Karnataka. As Chalukya power weakened in the second half of the 11th century, Vinayaditya and Ereyanga asserted their influence, though without renouncing Chalukya suzerainty. These Hoysala chiefs headed expeditions on behalf of the Chalukyas, repelling incursions from the

Yadavas, and even campaigning northwards into Malwa in central India to subdue the Paramara king. In 1062 Vinayaditya made his headquarters at Dvarasamudra (often Anglicised to Dorasamudra, but here referred to as Halebidu, the present-day name of the town). Here he constructed the vast reservoir, or "samudra" ("ocean"), which gave its name to the city.

Belur, Chennakeshava Temple, garlanded image of Vijayanarayana (Chennakeshava) worshipped in the sanctuary

Vishnuvardhana (r. 1108-42) was the first Hoysala to assert his autonomy by ceasing to send tribute to his Chalukya overlords. In 1117 he captured Talakadu in the extreme south of Karnataka, 165 kilometres from Halebidu. To celebrate this triumph over the Ganga feudatory of the Cholas who was based there, Vishnuvardhana performed purification rites and animal sacrifices, together with royal weighing and fire ceremonies. As a further act of commemoration, he erected temples to "Vishnu of Glory" (Kirtinarayana) at Talakadu and to "Vishnu of Victory" (Vijayanarayana) at Belur, 14 kilometres from Halebidu. After relocating his headquarters to Halebidu some five years later, Vishnuvardhana commissioned a grandly scaled temple with twin *linga* sanctuaries dedicated to himself and his principal queen. From here he consolidated his power by distributing coveted positions to his ministers, generals and governors, as well as to the Ganga, Chola and Pandya families of southern Karnataka and Tamil Nadu who accepted his leadership. He also proceeded northwards into the Chalukya domains from where he recruited skilled builders and artists. Vishnuvardhana is credited with inventing the fable about Sala, the mythical founder of the Hoysala lineage. This hero shielded a meditating Jain sage from a *yali*, or savage leonine beast, the sage crying "Hoy, Sala!" ("Strike, Sala!"). This legendary act of rescue was related by the Hoysalas in their poems and engraved records, and depicted as a royal motif in temple sculpture.

Belur, Chennakeshava Temple, Sala striking the savage beast

Under Narasimha I (r. 1142- 73) and Ballala II (r. 1173-1220), who between them governed for almost 80 years, new towns and settlements were established, as well as irrigation tanks, canals and wells, resulting in an unprecedented period of prosperity and territorial expansion. Ballala II challenged and defeated the Yadavas who had occupied the northern part of Karnataka, after which he styled himself as "Emperor of the South." Between them, these two kings supported numerous building projects and patronised the finest Kannada language poets of their day, like Janna and Nemichandra. Ballala II's son Narasimha II (r. 1220-35) began his career ruling the kingdom together with his father. During this time he headed successful expeditions against the Pandyas, forging alliances with the Cholas and thereby launching a permanent Hoysala presence in the Tamil country.

Someshvara (r. 1235-60), the succeeding monarch, inherited an affluent and prestigious realm. After resisting incursions by the Yadavas and Pandyas, he recovered territories previously lost in Tamil Nadu, making bequests to prominent temples along the lower course of the Kaveri. Conflict between Someshvara and his brother Narasimha III (r. 1254-92) offered opportunities for the Gajapatis of Orissa and the Yadavas to temporarily occupy the eastern and northern portions of the kingdom. Shortly after the next ruler Ballala III (r. 1292-1343) ascended to the Hoysala throne, peninsular India was invaded by Malik Kafur, commander of the troops of the Khalji sultans of Delhi. Devagiri, the Yadava citadel in the northern Deccan, capitulated in 1306, followed three years later by Warangal, headquarters of the Kakatiyas in the eastern Deccan. For a time, Ballala III shielded his domains from the conquerors, enlisting the support of his ministers and governors, especially those in the southern parts of his realm, to whom he granted a measure of independence.

Malik Kafur arrived in Halebidu in 1311, from where he took a large quantity of treasure and most of the royal elephants, before continuing into the Tamil country. After he had seized all the valuables, horses and elephants that he could, he returned to Delhi by way of Halebidu. Though Ballala III attempted an alliance with Malik Kafur, the Hoysala capital was vandalised and its great temple robbed. Ballala III sought refuge at Belur, but in 1316 was able to regain Halebidu and repair the damage. Ten years later, another army from Delhi, this time under the newly established Tughluq sultans, occupied the capital. Ballala III was compelled to retreat permanently to the Tamil country, where in 1340 he crowned his son as Ballala IV at Tiruvannamalai. Three years later he was killed in Madurai fighting the local Muslim governor. Ballala IV survived only until 1346.

During this turbulent era Harihara I emerged as a powerful individual. He was the son of Sangama, an officer who had served under Kampila, one of Ballala III's subordinates in the Tungabhadra valley region. In 1336 Harihara I declared his independence at his newly founded "City of Victory" (Vijayanagara) on the bank of the Tungabhadra river, claiming approval of the Hoysala monarch, who by this time had lost his Karnataka dominions. Together with his brother Bukka, Harihara I succeeded in expelling the Delhi invaders from the region. He then went on to incorporate most of the former Hoysala territories into the new, rapidly expanding kingdom of Vijayanagara, to which many former Hoysala commanders and governors shifted their allegiance. While later Vijayanagara rulers and their governors made bequests to the temple at Belur, a town that continued to thrive into later years, the Hoysala capital was eventually abandoned.

PATRONS AND ARTISTS

It was Vishnuvardhana, the first truly independent Hoysala, who was responsible for the great religious monuments at Belur and Halebidu described in this volume. The Vijayanarayana temple at Belur reflects the impact of the Shrivaishnava movement, believed to have been introduced into Karnataka by Ramanuja. This celebrated Tamil philosopher-teacher spent some 14 years in the Hoysala domains, meeting with the Hoysala king, who then changed his name from Bittideva to Vishnuvardhana. (There is even a tradition that Bittideva had originally been a Jain, and was converted by Ramanuja.) Thereafter this monarch made copious bequests to Shrivaishnava communities throughout his domains, providing generously for their sanctuaries and religious institutions. Even so, it was the Shiva temple at the capital of Halebidu that came to function as the preeminent dynastic monument. Its twin *linga* sanctuaries were dedicated to Vishnuvardhana as Hoysaleshvara, "Lord of the Hoysalas", and to his queen, Shantaladevi, under the name Shantaleshvara. Shantaladevi also acted as a patron, erecting the Kappe Chennigaraya temple (originally consecrated to Chennakeshava) next to her husband's great monument at Belur. In honour of this queen, who was Jain, Vishnuvardhana commissioned the the Shantinatha *basadi* at the Jain pilgrimage site of Shravanabelagola. Another royal female involved in temple construction is Abhinava Ketaladevi, the junior queen of Ballala II, responsible for the Kedareshvara temple in Halebidu.

Halebidu, Parshvanatha *basadi*, slab with Boppanna's foundation inscription

Apart from direct royal benefactions to religious monuments, Hoysala kings and queens also provided funds for this purpose to their ministers, generals and governors, sometimes even to their elite bodyguards and personal carriage-bearers. In contrast, the construction of Vishnuvardhana's great dynastic monument at Halebidu may have been financed in honour of the king entirely by Ketamalla, an influential merchant–officer.

Other figures at the time who benefitted from royal support included Boppanna, son of Gangaraja, one of Vishnuvardhana's ministers and commanders, who sponsored the Parshvanatha temple, the first of three Jain *basadis* to be erected at Halebidu. Another prominent minister was Perumalayadeva, who served under Someshvara, Narasimha III and Ballala III. This figure financed both Vaishnava and Shaiva monuments, together with *agraharas*, alms-houses, schools and reservoirs. Aimed at consolidating local loyalties, this pattern of sponsorship resulted in an astonishing number of more than 300 religious monuments being erected throughout the Hoysala kingdom in less than 150 years. Such a prolific dispersal of patronage testifies to the widespread networks of resources and political allegiances throughout Karnataka on which the Hoysala kings relied.

While newly founded Vishnu temples attest to the influence of Shrivaishnavism, most Hoysala temples are consecrated to Shiva. This affiliation accorded with the large and affluent Shaiva trading and agricultural communities of the kingdom, and the influence of prominent figures at the Hoysala court belonging to the Shaiva Pashupata, Lakulisha and Kalamukha sects. Ballala II is credited with contributing to more than 50 Shaiva temples and *mathas* during his almost 50-year reign. About 100 similar centres received support under Narasimha II, even though this ruler was not as a rule personally involved.

One of the most notable bequests by a later Hoysala ruler is that from Narasimha III to Somanatha Dandanayaka, an important minister and commander. Funds from the royal treasury permitted Somanatha to commission the splendid Keshava temple on the bank of the Kaveri, named after its patron at Somanathapura, 140 kilometres south of the capital. Here, too, Somanatha Dandanayaka installed five *lingas* to commemorate his family members. Naming religious monuments and their associated settlements after their sponsor, as in this instance, was customary in Hoysala times, though there was always a mention of the reigning monarch. Such acknowledgement gained permanence in inscriptions, such as those engraved on stone slabs set up at temple gateways or on the walls or doorways of the temples themselves.

In addition to evidence substantiating the role of Hoysala patrons, plentiful information is also available about individual sculptors, masons and scribes. This is in striking contrast with temples elsewhere in India, where most craftsmen are unacknowledged heroes. Label inscriptions on Hoysala carvings give the names, titles and affiliations of the workmen involved. Such data offer invaluable insight into the social and economic conditions of artists in Hoysala times. More than half of the 42 bracket figures in the Belur temple, for example, bear the names of different carvers, indicating the considerable number of specialists who had been assembled on this ambitious project. Some artists here, as well on other monuments, compare themselves to Vishvakarma, the legendary architect of the universe; others describe themselves as "destroyers" or "thunderbolts" to rival sculptors or calligraphers,

suggesting keen competition between them. Labels often specify the guilds to which the artists belonged, one of which called its members "Servants of Sarasvati", the goddess of knowledge, presumably their guardian divinity. The records often stipulate the payments and rewards that craftsmen earned, usually in the form of land grants or the right to collect dues.

One of the most famous Hoysala artists is Dasoja, who is first noticed at Belur, where he carved several bracket figures. Dasoja's name is also found at Halebidu and other sites, indicating that he travelled widely in response to different assignments. Suryana, one of the most popular and distinguished Hoysala scribes, was responsible for the inscription confirming Ballala II's additions at Belur. Mallitamma, another celebrated sculptor, was active for almost 60 years, travelling between projects all over the Hoysala kingdom. He ended his career at Somanathapura, where his name is found incised on the elephants of the temple plinth as well as on wall panels and even on one of the towers.

OPPOSITE
Belur, Chennakeshava Temple, bracket figure of maiden signed by Dasoja inside the *mandapa*

TEMPLE ARCHITECTURE

The expansion of the Hoysalas into northern Karnataka, and their campaigns beyond into Maharashtra and Malwa, as well as southward into the Tamil country, had its consequence in builders, masons and craftsmen moving from these zones to the new kingdom. Such migrations help explain the diversity of features in Hoysala architecture: the Dravida style imported from the Tamil zone; a Karnataka version of the Dravida style, inherited from the Chalukyas and perfected by the Hoysalas, here termed Vesara; and the Bhumija variant of the northern Indian Nagara style, as learned from the Yadavas and Paramaras. Notwithstanding, an essential ingredient of Hoysala architecture is the material out of which it is mostly realised; notably, locally available, grey-green chloritic schist (sometimes referred to as soapstone). Though comparatively soft, this stone was sufficiently robust to be used for columns up to 3.5 metres tall, and for beams spanning almost 4 metres across, and was the preferred medium for Hoysala builders. An exception was brick construction on a timber framework, sometimes used for towers over temple sanctuaries, as was common in the Tamil country. Vishnuvardhana adopted this technique for his monuments at Talakadu and Belur, possibly also at Halebidu, but this was not followed by his successors.

Halebidu, Hoysaleshvara Temple, east facade showing double entrances to the sanctuaries of king Vishnuvardhana (left) and queen Shantaladevi (right)

Hoysala temples fulfil the requirements essential for Hindu ritual practices. At the core is a sanctuary housing the deity to which the monument is dedicated, venerated by Brahmin priests on behalf of devotees. Sanctuaries to Shiva accommodate the phallic emblem of the divinity in the form of a *linga* elevated on a plinth; those consecrated to Vishnu enshrine a representation of the god in one of his many emanations or *avataras*. Adjoining the sanctuary is a small chamber, here referred to as a vestibule, where priests recite suitable prayers, conduct

Halebidu, Hoysaleshvara Temple, *linga* in the king's sanctuary

sacraments and convey offerings. Worshippers gather in a columned hall, or *mandapa*, in front, from where they can gaze into the sanctuary so as to benefit from an auspicious viewing of the deity within, known as *darshana*. *Mandapas* and their entrance porches vary in size and shape, but whatever their configuration, sanctuary, vestibule, *mandapa* and porch are invariably aligned along an axis that progresses towards zones of increasing sanctity, most often leading from east to west. A tower soaring above the sanctuary, its summit coinciding with the *linga* or image directly beneath, proclaims the presence of the deity within.

Hoysala temples present a considerable variety of layouts incorporating single, double or triple sanctuaries, as at Belur, Halebidu and Somanathapura, respectively. Each of the twin *linga* sanctuaries at Halebidu faces into a *mandapa*, and beyond, towards a free-standing Nandi pavilion, while those at Somanathapura accommodating different forms of Vishnu open from three sides into a common *mandapa*. Some Hoysala monuments even have five sanctuaries arranged in a long line, like the Panchalingeshvara at Somanathapura.

A distinctive aspect of Hoysala temples is the stellate plan, an attribute derived from Chalukya architecture. Sanctuaries at Belur, Halebidu and Somanathapura all have their walls divided into multiple facets with angled points. Such complex geometries are generated from squares rotated about a common point to create 16-sided configurations. However, not all 16 angles are expressed externally, since sanctuary walls adjoin *mandapas* and porches, or are partly obscured by outward-projecting subshrines, as at Belur and Halebidu. Some Hoysala sanctuaries are square in plan, but with multiple projections and recesses, the central projections being wider and more prominent, again in conformity with Chalukya practice. Both stellate and square layouts are combined in the Kedareshvara temple at Halebidu.

Larger Hoysala monuments, including those at Belur, Halebidu and Somanathapura, are elevated on plinths that create broad pathways for devotees to progress around the monument in a clockwise direction, known as *pradakshina*. Plinths have complicated outlines that echo temple layouts, including the stellate configurations just described. Sanctuary walls are raised on basement friezes that continue onto adjoining *mandapas*. Small subshrines inserted into the plinth, basement and sanctuary walls at Belur have Bhumija towers, with pyramidal tiers of tiny towered motifs interrupted by central tapering bands. (A full-scale

Bhumija tower of brick and plaster once rose above the Belur sanctuary.) In contrast, subshrines at Halebidu, including those inside the *mandapa*, are Vesara in style, with pyramidal, multi-storeyed towers topped by square-to-dome roofs known as *kutas*. (Possibly the towers over the twin sanctuaries at Halebidu were of the same type, but have subsequently disappeared.) Dravida towers are employed in the Panchalingeshvara at Somanathapura. Yet another tower type that occurs in Hoysala temples, here termed Phamsana, presents a pyramid of diminishing tiers of deeply cut horizontal mouldings, capped with a *kuta*. Mostly restricted to the Deccan region, Phamsana towers often appear in Hoysala architecture, as in the monuments of Halebidu town.

Sanctuary walls of Hoysala temples are treated elaborately. Those at Belur are divided into pillar-like projections topped with deeply

cut capitals. The faces of these projections as well as the intervening recesses are embellished with sculpted figures, topped with Bhumija towers or with looped frames, all in relief and sheltered by an overhang. Walls at Halebidu are formed almost entirely from sculpted panels set next to each other at angles, even bridging the corners. Sanctuary walls at Somanathapura are also covered with figural carvings, but these are mostly topped by Vesara towers that replicate those rising above the sanctuaries. In contrast, the Parshvanatha *basadi* at Halebidu is altogether plain, except for shallow projections bordered by pilasters.

Vesara towers of Hoysala temples present boldly modelled, diminishing tiers of miniature shrines with curved or vaulted roofs, reduced to block-like elements on low pilastered walls. Ornate horseshoe-arched motifs, known as *kudus*, embellish all these elements, while faceted, dome-like roofs are seen above. Superstructures have inward-facing projections with vault-like roofs fronted by enlarged arched motifs, as can be seen at Somanathapura.

Sanctuaries of Hoysala temples open into *mandapas* divided into columned bays, usually partly open as porches. Twin *mandapas* at Halebidu are each composed of nine bays, but linked by additional bays to achieve a grandly scaled interior; single-bay extensions on three sides serve as entrances. The Belur *mandapa*, the largest of all Hoysala columned halls, consists of 25 bays with broad central aisles in three directions ending in triple-bay porches. *Mandapas* in other Hoysala temples feature different arrangements of multiple bays with single- or triple-bay extensions. Such configurations often achieve symmetrical, *mandala*-like layouts. (Stellate shapes are only rarely encountered in *mandapas*, as in the 16-sided pavilion in front of the Shiva temple at Arsikere.)

Open porches of temple *mandapas* have stone seats with backrests. Tiny pilasters frame figural panels on their sloping outer surfaces at Belur and Halebidu, replaced by lines of relief temple towers at Somanathapura. Angled overhangs shelter the half-height columns raised on the balcony seats. At Belur and Halebidu the gaps between the porch columns were originally open, and only afterwards filled with stone screens with geometric perforations to admit light and air. The three entrances to the Belur *mandapa* comprise pairs of columns carrying elaborate pediments only, with doorways inserted later. In contrast, stone slabs carry ornate pediments over the entrances to the Halebidu temple.

OPPOSITE LEFT
Belur, Chennakeshava Temple, Bhumija model shrine beside the entrance steps

OPPOSITE RIGHT
Halebidu, Hoysaleshvara Temple, Vesara wall shrine inside the *mandapa*

Mandapa columns in Hoysala temples are showpieces of masonry technique. This is especially true of columns with circular shafts exhibiting curved profiles enlivened by precisely cut sharp incisions and ridges. The method of fashioning such columns out of chloritic schist is much debated. Most likely, stone blocks were placed vertically on a rotating base and then trimmed with metal wires, after which they were treated with an abrasive to attain a mirror-like polish. Other columns have square shafts with multiple facets; polygonal shafts with cut-out bands of foliation; or stellate shafts with sharply angled points. All these types are seen in the columns of the Belur *mandapa*. Horizontal ceilings inside *mandapas* are divided into compartments, or rise in corbelled rings to create dome-like interiors, often with pendant central lotuses surrounded by cut-out, timber-like ribs and rafters, and

Belur, Chennakeshava Temple, from southeast, columns inside the *mandapa*

even interweaving looped bands. The ceilings at Somanathapura are unsurpassed for their variety and virtuoso technique.

Hoysala monuments were not as a rule set in formally planned complexes. (The enclosure walls and entrance *gopura* at Belur are later additions.) The Halebidu temple was once approached from the south through a monumental gate, but this was mostly dismantled. The Somananthapura temple stands in a paved, walled courtyard entered through a gate with a *mandapa*-like interior, and lined with small shrines.

SCULPTURAL THEMES

Hoysala temples are unsurpassed for their wealth of images and dense ornamentation. The preoccupation with carved detail reflects the consummate skills of local artists, as well the possibilities of the chloritic medium in which they worked. This comparatively soft stone allowed a remarkable precision of detail, in spite of the rudimentary nature of the chisels with sharply angled and pointed ends of iron, possibly also of steel, with which the artists worked. Figures of divinities, consorts, celestials and humans are overwhelmed with encrusted costumes, jewels and hairstyles; the weapons, emblems and other attributes that they hold are similarly embellished. Hoysala art abounds in depictions of nature, as represented by elephants, horses, *hamsas* and imaginary creatures like leonine *yalis* and aquatic *makaras*, as well as trees, fruit-bearing plants and stylised leafy scrolls.

In addition to their obsession with detail, Hoysala artists were also concerned to fashion naturalistic male and female figures with sensitive facial expressions, fully rounded bodies, animated hand gestures and gracefully or dynamically disposed limbs. This sculptural realism is nowhere better expressed than in the depiction of the Sala legend. The heroic founder of the Hoysalas is shown clutching a dagger to stab a savage beast, described in contemporary literature as a tiger, but shown as a *yali*, with ferocious horns, eyes and mane, and curling tail. While portrayals of this combat flank the entrance steps at Belur, in temples elsewhere they are delegated to the roofs, from where they proclaim on high the supremacy of the Hoysalas. An example of this may be seen in one of the temples in Halebidu town. Further instances of naturalism in Hoysala sculpture are the magnificent seated Nandis in the pavilions in front of the *linga* sanctuaries at Halebidu, as well as the small, but majestic elephants punctuating the temple plinth at Somanathapura.

Basements of Hoysala temples are composed of superimposed friezes separated by deep incisions. Observant visitors may notice occasional unfinished carvings with chiselled outlines only; they suggest the haste by which blocks were assembled by different groups of workmen. The friezes depict animals, both real and imaginary; meandering leafy scrolls, sometimes inhabited by tiny figures and birds; and scenes depicting episodes from well known legends. Mythological compositions are generally positioned at eye level, so as to be more easily "read" by visitors as they proceed around the monument. Here are found familiar episodes from the *Ramayana, Bhagavata Purana*, *Mahabharata* and *Kiratarjuniya*. (*See page 140 for summaries of these stories.*) Basement narratives are arranged as linear friezes with scenes often merging into one another. Such compositions also portray contemporary life, in particular parades of royal elephants, horses and military contingents. Friezes at Halebidu and Somanathapura show soldiers bearing weapons in the company of elephants, horses, chariots and other trappings of war, all depicted with remarkable detail. Such realism offers invaluable insight into Hoysala martial culture.

Among the greatest masterpieces of Hoysala art are the brackets angling outwards from the tops of columns in temple porches and *mandapa* interiors fashioned in almost three dimensions as maidens posed beneath trees and foliage. (These figures are today usually called *madanikes*, but the craftsmen who signed the brackets referred to them as *shalabhanjikas* or *puttalis*.) These three-dimensional figures embody the ideal of female beauty, as expressed in a broad range of seductive images. At Belur, where the greatest number of such brackets is found, maidens appear as dancers playing musical instruments, huntresses bearing bows and arrows, or simply as young women admiring themselves in a mirror, plaiting their tresses, gazing at a parrot, or warding off a monkey. The sense of movement that animates these maidens is echoed in the swaying guardians set up beside *mandapa* entrances and vestibule doorways. Elaborately dressed and armed with clubs, these figures are posed in gorgeous frames that emphasise

Halebidu, Hoysaleshvara Temple
OPPOSITE basement friezes

BELOW detail of guardian figure beside vestibule doorway

Halebidu, Hoysaleshvara Temple, wall panel of Shiva dancing inside the skin of the elephant demon

their significant function as protectors of sacred monuments.

Ornamented pediments over the entrances at Belur and Halebidu show deities set in copious foliation issuing from open-mouthed *makaras* with fantastic scrolling tails at either side. Stone screens at Belur incorporate relief panels portraying the patron of the monument together with his ministers, officers, attendants and principal queens. Such compositions offer unique visual testaments of formal audiences at the Hoysala court. Here too are found the narratives of Vamana and of Krishna, and particularly of Narasimha savagely killing Hiranyakashipu in retribution for tormenting Prahlada, the son of Hiranyakashipu. The latter scene is accorded a particular significance in Hoysala art, since it is also depicted on a doorway pediment and wall panel at Belur, as well as on the angled backrests flanking the *mandapa* doorway at Somanathapura.

Walls of sanctuaries and *mandapas* of the temples included in this volume are covered with sculpted divinities. At Belur these include a comprehensive range of Vishnu's *avataras* and emanations, expressing the Shrivaishnava emphasis on the worship of Vishnu in his manifold manifestations. The same is true at Somanathapura, though here Ganesha and Durga are also included. A greater mix of Shaiva and Vaishnava divinities is seen at Halebidu. Gods stand in formal postures, or are seated calmly with their consorts, like Vishnu with Lakshmi, or Shiva with Parvati. But they also appear in violent moods, not only as Narasimha, who has already been mentioned, but also as Shiva dancing triumphantly in the skin of the elephant demon that he has just slaughtered, or forcefully spearing a crawling, dwarf. Other dynamic portrayals include Garuda flying through the air, Krishna holding up Govardhana to shelter the herds, and Ravana shaking Kailasa.

In contrast to the sculptural exuberance of their exteriors, interiors of Hoysala temples are austere. Ornamentation is mostly restricted to columns, some with figures angling from brackets high up, and elaborate pediments over vestibule doorways flanked by guardians. Ceilings are divided into compartments, filled with lotuses, but also with divinities in the company of all eight Dikpalas. Magnificent icons of presiding deities, almost human in size and fashioned in three dimensions are installed in temple sanctuaries. Those at Belur are still venerated, and are so decorated that they can hardly be viewed, unlike the magnificent icons of Janardhana and Venugopala at Somanathapura. Such imposing sculptures testify to the ability of Hoysala artists to create monumental images imbued with divine power. The same is even true of the much smaller icons of various gods and goddesses in the wall shrines within the *mandapa* of the Kappe Chennigaraya temple at Belur. Here too we should mention the images of Parshvanatha and Shantinatha in the Jain *basadis* at Halebidu, which are by far the largest figural carvings of the era. That of Parshvanatha portrays the naked Tirthankara standing majestically in front of a cobra.

Somanathapura, Keshava Temple, image of Venugopala in the south sanctuary

Chennakeshava Temple, east entrance

BELUR

For most visitors to Belur today the principal attraction is the great Chennakeshava temple founded in 1117 by the Hoysala king Vishnuvardhana to commemorate his victory over the Cholas at Talakadu. This magnificent temple stands in a high walled, paved courtyard measuring 135 by 120 metres, entered from the east through a lofty *gopura* on axis with the temple itself, 30 metres beyond. Vishnuvardhana's queen Shantaladevi commissioned the Kappe Chennigaraya temple immediately south of the Chennakeshava, and it was probably Vishnuvardhana's grandson Ballala II who financed the Viranarayana temple to the west. All the other buildings in the courtyard, including the *gopura*, belong to later periods, even though many incorporate reused Hoysala stone pieces. An exception is the stepped tank in the northeast corner, which is credited to Ballala II. (*See inside front jacket for a schematic map of the whole complex.*)

The chronological range of these features at Belur alludes to a town that continued to flourish as a pilgrimage centre with a significant Hindu monument well after the demise of the Hoysalas. During these years the Chennakeshava was subjected to numerous repairs, and in time became surrounded with lesser shrines and subsidiary structures. Ministers and governors of the Vijayanagara emperors who assumed control of this part of Karnataka by the middle of the 14th century ordered many of these additions, followed some 200 years later by a local line of Nayakas. Interest in the Chennakeshava continued under the Wodeyars of Mysuru, who incorporated Belur into their domains in the course of the 17th century. In the early years of the 20th century, Krishnaraja Wodeyar IV presented the temple with a bronze statuette of himself in devotional attitude (now displayed in the Devasthanam Office). At the same time, the Mysore Archaeological Department carried out substantial repairs, including the demolition of nearby dilapidated structures. The temple now comes under the Archaeological Survey of India, but worship continues, attracting crowds of devotees, especially during the festival for Keshava that takes place in April. In recent years a music and dance programme has been staged in March.

GOPURA, DHVAJASTAMBHA AND *DIPASTAMBHA*

Visitors entering the towered gate of the temple complex will at first observe a number of features as they progress towards the Chennakeshava temple.

See photograph on page 1

Gopura The brightly painted yellow tower of the gate, clearly visible at the western terminus of Belur's main commercial street, dominates the entire temple complex. The *gopura* rises on a lower, granite structure with a double series of shallow pilastered projections, interrupted by a central passageway. The steeply pyramidal tower of brick and plaster has four diminishing storeys capped with a barrel-vaulted roof with arched ends and five brass-clad pot finials. Doorway jambs within the passageway show maidens grasping creepers, but the carving is mostly unfinished. Typical of 16th-century religious architecture, the *gopura* is a project of a Vijayanagara governor, probably replacing one or more earlier gates dating back to Hoysala times.

Dhvajastambha and Garuda Immediately inside the *gopura* stands a 7-metre high *dhvajastambha*, from which banners are unfurled on special occasions. Its wooden column has been re-clad in gleaming brass sheets, those at the cubical base embossed with Vaishnava *naman*, disc, conch and kneeling Garuda.

A schist statue of Garuda placed in front of the *dhvajastambha* faces towards the Chennakeshava temple. Fashioned as a human figure with bird-like nose, outstretched wings and human hands brought together in salutation, this eagle *vahana* of Vishnu stands within an ornate frame. It is attributed to Javaracharya, an early-20th-century artist from Mysuru. The adjacent stone altar has a square moulded base with a carved, petalled top.

Dipastambha A 10-metre high *dipastambha* added by a Vijayanagara period governor stands freely some 30 metres southwest of the *dhvajastambha*. Raised on a plinth with indented sides, its slender, octagon-to-16-sided granite shaft preserves a double capital, but has lost its topmost metal lamp-holder.

CHENNAKESHAVA TEMPLE

Before describing the temple's architecture and sculptures it is worth considering the circumstances of its foundation and subsequent history.

Historical Context An extremely long inscription inside the temple *mandapa* gives an account of the rise of the Hoysalas, including the legend of Sala, before listing the achievements, titles and epithets of Vishnuvardhana. It then continues: "When this king was in his residence in the great city of Velapura [Belur], ruling his kingdom

Chennakeshava Temple, from southeast

in peace and wisdom, he set up with faith the god Vijayanarayana at a specified date [equivalent to 20th March 1117] to provide for daily ceremonies, decorations and offerings at three times to Vijayanarayana, Chennakeshava and Lakshminarayana." From this statement it is clear that the main temple at Belur was originally consecrated to Vijayanarayana and only later did this deity come to be worshipped as Chennakeshava, the name by which it is known today. The other two gods mentioned in the inscription received veneration in the adjacent Kappe Chennigaraya temple.

Among the later Hoysalas who made contributions to the Chennakeshava is Ballala II. Towards the end of the 12th century he commissioned the "latticed windows, secure door frames, door lintels, kitchen, ramparts, pavilion and Vasudeva *tirtha*". The woodwork of the brick tower over the sanctuary was repaired in 1298 by Somanatha Dandanayaka, the trusted general of Ballala III, who was also the patron of the temple at Somanathapura. Further alterations were carried out in 1387 by Kampanna, minister of the Vijayanagara emperor Harihara II, and then again in 1736 by Venkata, a local ruler, and in 1744 by a governor of Haidar Ali of Mysuru.

Layout In spite of these successive campaigns of restorations, the Chennakeshava preserves its original layout. The east-facing sanctuary, which accommodates the principal cult image of Vishnu, is of the stellate type, but only the intermediate angles of its 16-sided plan are evident, since subshrines protrude from three sides of its outer walls. A square vestibule serves as a transition to the *mandapa* in front. This hall has 25 bays, with triple-bay extensions on the north, east and south. These create a stepped plan measuring almost 35 metres north-south and 28 metres east-west, making it the largest enclosed space in all Hoysala architecture. The frontal (eastern) half of the *mandapa* was originally conceived as a part-open porch, with high balcony seating all around and broad entryways on three sides, at B, G and L. (*These and other letters giving locations are indicated on the plan on page 38.*) Only under Ballala II were stone screens and doorways added to close off the interior.

The temple is elevated on a broad plinth some 4 metres wide. This completely surrounds the building, echoing the stepped plan of its *mandapa* and stellate angles of its sanctuary. As they proceed around the temple visitors may notice iron clamps securing the outer blocks

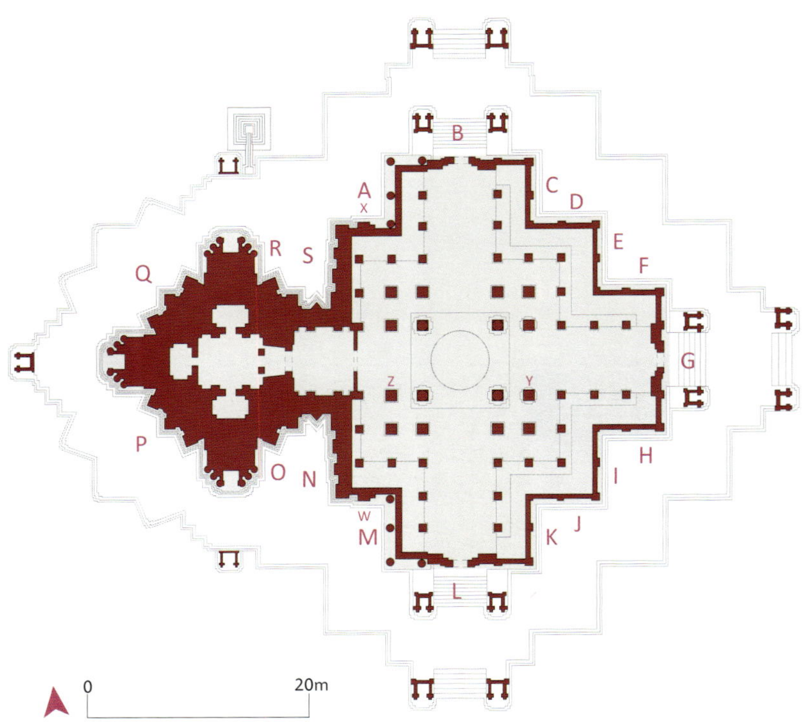

A
B
C
D
E
F
G
H
I
J
K
L
M
N
O
P
Q
R
S
X
W
Z
Y
0
20m

of the plinth, as well as a pair of footprints, popularly believed to be those of Vishnu, etched into the plinth to the north of the vestibule (S). The plinth is raised 1.2 metres above the pavement on three sharply cut, unadorned courses. They are interrupted on three sides by access steps flanked by subshrines at pavement level (B, G and L). Identical subshrines flank the second flights of steps at plinth level, which lead to the three *mandapa* entrances. Additional subshrines of the same type are placed against the plinth, aligned with those protruding from the sanctuary itself.

***Mandapa* Subshrines and Basement** Subshrines beside the steps just noticed present in miniature form a complete temple elevation. Those at pavement level have cubical chambers (now mostly empty) flanked by pilasters with tiny guardian figures, maidens and leaping *yalis*. Side walls exhibit a variety of geometric designs with diamond-shaped flowers, occasionally with perforations. Doorways are overhung by angled eaves, and topped by pyramidal square towers of

OPPOSITE
Chennakeshava Temple, plan

BELOW
Northeast corner of *mandapa* porch

the Bhumija type, with tapering bands in the middle of four sides flanked by tiers of diminutive towers. Subshrines at plinth level are raised on a continuation of the basement course of elephants that runs around the temple, together with a scroll frieze. Otherwise, they resemble the subshrines at pavement level, except the Bhumija towers which have stellate plans and are topped with *amalakas* and vase pinnacles.

The exterior of the *mandapa* porch is carried on a sequence of superimposed friezes some 3.3 metres high. These run between the three entrances to the temple, up to the buttress-like projections indicating the limits of the original open portions of the temple (W and X). The lowest courses show parades of elephants, the animals proceeding towards the corners; a curved moulding with diamond-shaped flowers; a cornice with garlands beneath and *kudus* with raised *kirtimukhas* above; continuous creeper motif, with tiny musicians, dancers and other figures worked into the scrolls, and *kirtimukhas* at the outer corners; and inverted cornice with a frieze of garlands.

The upper basement courses of the porch present a profusion of sharply modelled details. The first of these has cut-out, projecting niches with looped garlands or foliation framing tiny male and female dancers and musicians, as well as Ganesha, Virabhadra, Vishnu, Garuda, etc. Seated, pot-bellied *yakshas* and other figures occupy the intervening recesses. The next course comprises regularly spaced, shallow faceted pilasters with occasional figures in between. This is topped with an overhanging eave with pendant garlands, with miniature Bhumija temple towers alternating with additional, tiny cut-out figures above.

The porch basement's topmost course coincides with the sloping backrest of the balcony seating. This is divided by pairs of colonettes into panels filled with Narasimha, Vishnu on Ananta, Hanuman, Bhairava, dancing Shiva and other deities, as well as dancers, musicians and amorous couples, with prancing *yalis* at the corners. Of particular interest are the *Mahabharata* episodes portrayed in more than 20 panels running in an anti-clockwise sequence, from left to right (I and H). The narrative begins with the fateful game of dice, in which Yudhishthira loses his kingdom to the Kauravas, after which the Pandavas have to retire to the forest. Here rivalry breaks out between the two families, with Bhima shaking the diminutive Kauravas out of a tree. Then follow scenes of the exiled Pandavas in the service of king Virata: notably, the Kaurava raid of Virata's cows; the fights between the Pandavas and

Mandapa porch backrest panels

TOP
Amorous couples

MIDDLE
Scenes from the *Mahabharata*

BOTTOM
Wrestling match

Kauravas; and Arjuna returning Virata's cows. The preparations for battle that follow show the councils of the Pandavas and Kauravas; Bhishma and his troops setting out to war; the fight between Arjuna and Bhishma; Bhishma dying on a bed of arrows; Bhima struggling with Supratika, the giant elephant of his enemy Bhagadatta; and finally Bhima being rescued by Arjuna.

Visitors should seek out a trio of panels next to the south *mandapa* entrance that depicts a sporting match (M). A couple seated beneath parasols, probably courtiers, as well as spectators, all gaze towards a pair of interlocked wrestlers.

***Mandapa* Screens and Entrances** Slender columns with part circular shafts exhibiting multiple incisions are placed at regular intervals around the open, porch portions of the *mandapa* (B to L). The columns carry the double-curved overhanging eave that runs continually around the *mandapa*. Perforated screens inserted by Ballala II fill what would have been gaps between the columns. The screens have lines of stepped square perforations, but also incorporate bands of scrollwork and relief panels portraying scenes of royal audience as well as mythological narratives. (*They are described in the Appendix on page 62.*)

The entrances on three sides of the *mandapa* were originally broad openings spanned by beams almost 4 metres across. Set within these openings are pairs of free-standing columns with part-circular columns and circular and square capitals. These carry elaborate

East entrance

pediments that barely touch the beams above, providing no structural support. Each pediment shows kneeling Garuda carrying an aspect of Vishnu set in an intricately worked frame: Keshava between Bhu and Lakshmi, with female attendants on the north (B); Narasimha disembowelling Hiranyakashipu on the east (G); and on the south (L), an almost identical figure of multi-armed Varaha disembowelling Hiranyaksha, sometimes considered the brother of Narasimha's victim. The figures are contained within arches of filigree scrollwork and looped garlands of remarkable delicacy headed by *kirtimukhas*. The arches issue from open-mouthed *makaras* with tiny riders at either side. These creatures have extravagant tails that originally swirled upwards only.

ABOVE Floral panel beside south entrance

FOLLOWING PAGES *Mandapa* porch, bracket figures; *see also photographs on pages 4 and 5*

Ballala II is credited with adding slabs to fill in the openings on either side of the columns. These are carved with the downward swirls of *makara* tails, as well as panels with varied floral designs, including lines of blossoms and pendant leafy bunches in high relief; guardians holding staffs or clubs are seen beneath. The modifications also include doorway frames inserted clumsily between the columns. Figures at the base of the jambs show female attendants with fly-whisks on the north (B); Manmatha and Rati on the east (G); and Hanuman and Garuda on the south (L). Ballala II may also have been responsible for commissioning the pairs of three-dimensional representations of Sala placed beside each entrance. The kneeling hero is shown here vigorously attacking a ferocious *yali* by raising a dagger to strike the beast (at G and L), clutching the animal's ear, or resisting a claw thrust upon his head (at B).

See photograph on page 14

***Mandapa* Brackets** The artistic highlight of the Chennakeshava is undoubtedly the series of brackets portraying 35 maidens and three male figures. These cut-out figures angle outwards from blocks projecting from the upper square capitals of the *mandapa* porch columns. (Four similar brackets inside the hall are noticed below). Unrivalled for their depiction of dance and music, and evocation of

female beauty, these maidens have miraculously escaped damage, as have the intricately worked leafy bowers and creepers beneath which they are so alluringly posed. Chavana, Dasoja and Malloja are among the artists who engraved their names and boastful titles on the bases of the brackets.

Beginning with the brackets over the *mandapa's* north entrance (B), we encounter a maiden with a hunting weapon, one of her attendants carrying the prey; two dancers, one with the hands held above the head and across the waist; and a unique naked figure, shaking out her garment, presumably to rid it of the scorpion shown near to her foot. Continuing in a clockwise direction around the *mandapa*, maidens are portrayed clutching a palm-leaf book; holding a fan and a folded betel leaf in her two hands (C); rubbing the string of a *vina* with a stick; holding up one hand in a dance gesture (D); pretending to play the flute; dancing with a tiny drum; and holding up a stick to drive away a bothersome, diminutive monkey (E). This sequence ends with a dancer balancing on one foot, while an attendant tries to fix a ring to one of her toes; and yet another male drummer.

Continuing with the four brackets above the *mandapa's* east entrance (G): from right to left, these depict a musician about to strike tiny cymbals; a dancer with one arm extended outwards; a maiden gazing wistfully into a circular mirror; and another holding a parrot, as if listening to the love message which the bird conveys. Continuing in a clockwise direction around the *mandapa*, we notice maidens in an angry mood, with the legs crossed; holding up a branch to strike a mischievous monkey clutching her garment; in a striding posture, holding up a bow and aiming an arrow (I); squeezing out water from a long tress of hair after a bath; holding up a small drum in the act of pacing out a dance (J); and beating a drum with the right hand; next to which is a male flautist (K). This sequence ends with the brackets above the south entrance (L) showing maidens singing, dancing, strumming a fretted musical instrument, and checking in a mirror to adjust her hair. In the adjacent face (M) we find a huntress wearing a leafy skirt, aiming her bow up high. Another male drummer is carved onto the bracket in the rear internal corner.

Outer Walls and Sculpture Panels The vestibule, *mandapa* and sanctuary walls are in a noticeable different style and proportionate system from the open, porch portions of the *mandapa*. Running around the western half of the temple from the plain, buttress-like projections at W and X, the walls rise upon a basement with a bottom course of elephant parades that continues that from beneath the porch. Widely spaced, tiny model shrines with Bhumija towers in shallow relief adorn the sharply modelled courses above.

Full-height columns with multi-faceted shafts and capitals mark the midpoints of the vestibule walls. Elsewhere, the walls are composed entirely from pillar-like projections arranged in a row at the rear of the *mandapa*, and as single units set at angles to each other on the stellate sanctuary. The projections are embellished with sculpted deities set between pairs of slender pilasters carrying frames of looped garlands, or pyramidal towers of the Bhumija or Vesara type in high relief. Recesses between the pillar-like projections also accommodate deities, but these are carved against single pilasters topped with similar temple towers. Variant stellate shafts and capitals of the half-pillars on the north and south walls mark the junction of the vestibule and sanctuary within.

The most frequent wall sculptures depict Vishnu seated with Lakshmi, or standing alone, holding the usual conch and disc. Here we draw attention to the more unusual and visually arresting icons, listing them in a clockwise sequence beginning on the walls to the left of the *mandapa's* south entrance (L). In the first two series (N and O): Harihara, with a diminutive Nandi on the left and Garuda on the right; Shiva lifting up Jalandhara on the point of his trident, while the demon attempts to supplicate the god; skeletal Kali, her many arms displaying an assortment of vicious weapons; Vamana as an almost naked mendicant holding an umbrella; and Ravana with multiple heads and arms lifting up Kailasa, the mountain crowded with tiny figures, animals and trees, with Shiva with Parvati seated on top.

The following series (P) begins with Durga spearing Mahisha, the latter shown as a human torso emerging out of the decapitated buffalo body. Then comes triple-headed, bearded Brahma holding noose, water-pot, rosary and ritual ladle. One of the angled blocks that follows is carved with a pair complimentary, aggressive figures: Narasimha disembowelling his victim, with the entrails gruesomely displayed; and Shiva dancing in the skin of the elephant demon that he has just slaughtered, with diminutive witnesses at either side. Then comes Bhikshatana as the naked wanderer, clutching a decapitated head and wearing sandals. Here too is an unusual icon of Surya, now missing

FOLLOWING PAGES
Narasimha and dancing Shiva wall panels

ABOVE Brahma and Bhikshatana wall panels

OPPOSITE Subshrine on south side of sanctuary

the chariot in which he rides, except for the horses beneath. While the next panels (Q) are mostly of standing deities found elsewhere, several in the last two series (R and S) are unique: they include Varaha rescuing Bhudevi, with the prostate figure of the demon below; Manmatha holding a curvaceous, sugarcane bow, accompanied by Rati; and Arjuna winning Draupadi's hand by aiming his arrow at a fish target atop a pillar, while gazing at its reflection in a bowl of water beneath.

Subshrines The wall scheme with its sequence of sculpted icons just described is interrupted by double-storey subshrines on stepped plans projecting outwards from three sides of the main sanctuary. The lower storeys rise on basement mouldings with elephant parades beneath, and lines of *yalis* and horse-riders above. Then come friezes of creepers or rows of tiny temple towers, and miniature inclined balconies with diminutive figural panels between cut-out pairs of pilasters, with central gaps for spouts (mostly missing). Jambs with miniature guardians bearing clubs frame the doorways of the subshrines accommodating icons of Vishnu. Side walls between faceted and stellate colonettes are

enlivened with carvings of deities or diamond-shaped flowers motifs.

Overhanging eaves provide the transition to the smaller, upper storeys of the subshrines, now empty. These repeat the balconies, doorways and side walls from beneath, but with the addition of stellate, model Bhumija towers complete with pot finials in the rear corners. Ornate eaves with occasional miniature figures are surmounted by pyramidal Vesara towers with *kuta* roofs and vase finials. These reach the main eave that runs around the entire temple, thereby integrating the subshrines with the building's overall elevation.

The Missing Tower Visitors to Belur can hardly fail to notice that the exterior of the Chennakeshava lacks a vertical ascent in the form of a tower rising above its sanctuary. That such a tower once existed is confirmed by records that mention its repairs from 1298 onwards, up until its demolition in the 1880s by the Mysore Archaeological Department, leaving not a trace. From these notices we learn that the tower was built of brick on a timber support, though we doubt whether the tower in the early photographs dates from the Hoysala

Brick tower in 1869: photograph by Edmund David Lyon (Courtesy British Library)

era. That said, its Bhumija style, with tapering bands in the middle of four faces flanked by diminishing tiers of model towers, resembles the towers of the subshrines beside the flights of steps at the temple's three entrances. Judging from these examples, as well as the towers of other designs elsewhere in Hoysala architecture, superstructures rising upon sanctuaries are rarely much taller than the heights of the walls. From this point of view, the tower at Belur in the early photographs is out of proportion, leading us to conclude that it was a later, crudely built replacement.

(Here we note that the adjacent Kappe Chennigaraya and Viranarayana temples are also missing their towers, which may also have been of brick and then dismantled.)

Interior On entering the *mandapa* through the east or south doorways (that on the north is usually closed) visitors will be amazed at the spaciousness of the Chennakeshava's high-ceilinged interior. However, this is somewhat dimly lit, making it difficult to see the lengthy foundation inscription of Vishnuvardhana engraved onto the walls to the left (west) of the north entrance (B). Shorter inscriptions on columns record additions to the temple by later Hoysala rulers and their successors.

The much wider spans between the central lines of columns running east-west and north-south result in three broad aisles converging on the bay in front of the main sanctuary. Four columns here stand on a raised floor area inscribed with a circle. Cubical blocks at the column bases have sharp mouldings interrupted by tiny figures of Vishnu in ornate frames accompanied by dancers and maidens. The impressive part-circular, lathe-turned shafts of the columns have sharply worked incisions and rims, as well as friezes of jewelled garlands in delicate relief. Capitals are of the circular and projecting square type embellished with friezes of garlands. Four sculpted maidens angle outwards over the central bay: two portray dancers; the others show maidens wringing out her hair, and holding a bird with a peacock-like tail on her elbow. Of consummate workmanship, the figures rival the naturalism and grace of the outer brackets of the temple; like these, the maidens are posed beneath cut-out, leafy foliage. The artists Chavana and Dasoja signed two of the brackets.

See photograph on page 26

See photograph on page 18

Higher brackets with angled undersides carry the beams and great dome-like ceiling measuring more than 3.5 metres in diameter

Mandapa interior
ABOVE
Central dome-like ceiling

OPPOSITE
"Narasimha" column

that soars over the central *mandapa* bay. The ceiling has three concentric corbelled rings of tiny Vaishnava figures encircling a one-metre hanging block carved with Narasimha killing Hiranyakashipu.

Next to the *mandapa's* four central columns are two supports, which attracted the virtuoso skills of the Hoysala stone carvers. The so-called Narasimha column (Y on the plan; *see page 38*) has a 12-sided shaft that is almost entirely concealed by tiers of cut-out miniature shrines housing standing figures of Vishnu. (The idea that column somehow once rotated may be dismissed.) Its cubical base has relief panels showing multi-headed Ravana beneath Shiva and Parvati (east), Shiva spearing Andhaka, and shooting arrows at the demons of the triple cities (north), and the gods and demons churning the cosmic ocean (south). Angled miniature figures embellish the brackets above. Another nearby column has a full relief female, popularly identified as Mohini, on its eastern face (Z on the plan; *see photograph on page 8*). She is depicted with a serene expression and a sinuous body with prominent breasts and narrow waist. Elaborately dressed, jewelled and crowned, Mohini stands within a prominent frame of looped garlands carried on shallow pilasters, suggesting that she may be a goddess. Since her two hands carrying emblems are lost, no certain identification is possible. The faceted shaft behind is almost totally concealed by eight vertical bands of perforated scrolls. They contain foliate tufts and buds, *yalis* and tiny figures including a complete set of Dikpalas and of Vishnu's *avataras*.

Immediately in front of the Mohini column is the vestibule doorway giving access to Keshava's sanctuary. This is flanked by imposing guardian figures of almost human size, complete in all the details of their costumes, jewellery and crowns, as well as the conch, disc and mace held in the hands, and the clubs on which they lean. Tiny female attendants with fly-whisks are seen beneath at the side, and the usual frames of looped garlands to the rear. The doorway between the guardians has a lintel with perforated floral garlands and diminutive musicians on its underside. This carries an intricately worked pediment showing Keshava seated with Lakshmi within an arch of scrollwork. The arch is framed by looped garlands issuing from open-mouthed *makaras* with the usual extravagant tails fanning upwards and outwards.

Pediment over vestibule doorway

The doorway at the rear of the vestibule has decorated jambs and lintel, and small guardian figures beneath at either side. Through its opening, beyond a pair of free-standing columns, visitors may glimpse the commanding, standing image of the temple deity. More than 2.5 metres high, Keshava is elevated on a pedestal, but is almost totally concealed by cloths, garlands and embossed brass fittings. Even so, the conch and disc can be made out in the god's rear hands, with lotus in the front right hand, and club beneath the left arm. A smaller metal statue, also garlanded, is placed in the vestibule, from where it is taken in procession at festival times.

See photograph on page 13

Columns elsewhere in the *mandapa* exhibit inventive designs. Two in the east aisle have octagonal shafts embellished with tiers of elegant, pointed leaves and blossoms. Columns in the south aisle are arranged in pairs with octagonal-, 16- and 32-sided shafts and capitals as they progress inwards from the south entrance. The flutings and angles of the columns rise through friezes of buds and jewels. Such supports contrast with more usual circular and faceted columns standing free of the *mandapa* walls, embedded in the one-metre high balcony, reached by narrow flights of steps, or set between the perforated screens above the angled backrests.

Apart from the ceiling over the central bay, those roofing many of the other bays of the *mandapa* are enhanced with rows of lotus blossoms. The three bays immediately inside each entrance, however, have ceilings divided into compartments with medallions containing Keshava (north), Narasimha (east) and Varaha (south), as on the pediments over the entrances on these particular sides. These ceiling deities are each surrounded by sets of Dikpalas on their animal mounts, always correctly oriented so that Indra on the elephant and Yama on the buffalo, for instance, are positioned on the east and south respectively.

Among the curiosities to be seen in the south aisle of the *mandapa* is a glass case containing an extraordinary pair of gigantic leather sandals donated some years ago by local cobblers. A brightly gilded *vahana* in the semblance of a coiled cobra with a rearing hood is also displayed here. Carved onto the topmost course of the raised balcony behind the glass case is the only set of *Ramayana* panels found on the temple. They begin on the right with the council of war between Rama and Lakshmana and the monkey army, and end on the left with Hanuman and the monkeys carrying boulders to build the causeway to Lanka.

Appendix: Screen Panels on the Chennakeshava Temple

Either side of the east entrance to the *mandapa* (G), the panels depict scenes of royal audience showing the same bearded figure holding a long sword. These are likely to be portraits of Ballala II, who was responsible for adding the screens. The Hoysala monarch is shown seated in the company of his principal queen and her retinue, together with his officers (right-hand panel), or brahmin advisors and their disciples (left-hand panel). Narasimha or Keshava between Hanuman and Garuda are depicted above.

See photograph on pages 10-11

Screen panels on the north side of the *mandapa* begin with that to the left of the north entrance (B). This shows Hanuman and Garuda fighting over what looks like a *linga* splitting into two halves, out of which Shiva might perhaps miraculously appear, even though the scene is presided above by Vishnu and Lakshmi. Vishnu asleep on Ananta occupies the central panel in the next screen (C). The following screen presents an abbreviated versionof the *Bhagavata Purana* (D). Krishna plays the flute attended by cows and herdsmen in the bottom register; above, Krishna slays the elephant demon, and wins a wrestling match

Screen panel (B)

against the champion Chanura; the climax of the action occurs in the top register, where Krishna pulls the wicked king Kamsa down from his throne. Gods and demons tugging at Vasuki's long serpent tail in the act of churning the cosmic ocean replace one creeper strip on the next screen (E).

Screen panels on the south side of the *mandapa* begin with the story of Trivikrama (H). The bottom register shows Bali making his gift to Vamana. In the middle register, Vamana, now transformed into Trivikrama, paces out the earth; to the right Garuda drags away Bali's evil minister. The top register has Vishnu and Lakshmi flanked by Hanuman and Garuda. The next two screens (K) show Krishna dancing on Kaliya, with musicians below; and the Dikpalas riding on their respective animal mounts, in the company of Shiva and Parvati on Nandi above, and armed warriors below. The last screen to the right of the south entrance (L) relates the story of Prahlada: the bottom register depicts the youth resisting the torments of a trampling elephant, armed guard, writhing serpents and flames; Narasimha disembowels Hiranyakashipu in the register above.

Screen panel (H)

KAPPE CHENNIGARAYA TEMPLE

Shantaladevi commissioned this temple in 1117, at the same time as her lord Vishnuvardhana erected the monument immediately to the north. The Kappe Chennigaraya is of the *dvikuta* type, with two sanctuaries on the west and south originally dedicated to Chennakeshava and Lakshminarayana respectively. The sanctuaries open into a *mandapa* with four columns in the middle, extended as triple-bayed porches to the east and north, thereby creating a stepped layout. As in the adjacent Chennakeshava temple, the gaps between the porch columns were later filled in with stone screens and doorways, perhaps also at the instigation of Ballala II.

The Kappe Chennigaraya is raised on a broad plinth that repeats the *mandapa* porch projections, as well as the outlines of the stellate plan of the west sanctuary and square plan of the south sanctuary. Double

flights of steps flanked by elephants climb to the temple on both the east and north. A diminutive pond imitating a stepped well is set into the pavement to the north. This is to take libations from the spout on the west sanctuary.

The temple presents a somewhat severe, boldly articulated exterior devoid of carvings. Basement courses around the porch portions of the *mandapa* are surmounted by the angled backrest of the balcony seating, enlivened with diamond-shaped motifs. Screens with geometric perforations between circular columns flank doorways with small guardian figures at the base of the jambs. Sanctuary walls rise on a different set of basement courses, occasionally relieved by small towered niches. The walls are formed from pillar-like projections with sharp incisions on their shafts and capitals, set at angles to each other on the stellate faces of the west sanctuary. Subshrines with *kuta* roofs are placed on the axial faces to

Kappe Chennigaraya Temple, from northeast

accommodate Vishnu images, though these are later replacements. While the walls all around the building are overhung by a sharp eave, there is no evidence of towers above either of the sanctuaries.

Four columns with part-circular, lathe-turned shafts define the central bay of the *mandapa*. Projecting blocks above, carved with flying male figures support three angled brackets fashioned as female drummers and a maiden holding a lotus; the fourth bracket is missing. These are comparable in style and quality to the brackets in the Chennakeshava temple. The ceiling above has roundels containing Vishnu and Lakshmi surrounded by the Dikpalas mounted on their respective animals. The adjacent ceiling shows blossoms surrounding a dancing image of Vishnu, with a curious frieze of interlocking *yalis* carved onto the supporting beams. Imposing guardians bearing Vaishnava attributes flank the west vestibule doorway. This is surmounted by a lintel with figures of Vishnu and Lakshmi seated within an ornate frame, between *makaras* disgorging looped garlands. Beyond is the 2-metre high stone image of Chennakeshava cloaked in cloths and garlands; an inscription on its base states that it was set up by queen Shantaladevi. A panel showing Narasimha disembowelling Hiranyakashipu surmounts the south vestibule doorway. The Venugopala icon enshrined within, however, is not original, unlike the images in the wall shrines beside both vestibule doorways. Visitors should seek out these modestly sized, but finely worked images of Ganesha, Sarasvati holding the noose and book, Vishnu with Lakshmi, and Durga spearing the buffalo.

Kappe Chennigaraya Temple, west vestibule

LEFT
Kappe Chennigaraya Temple, Sarasvati and Durga inside the *mandapa*

BELOW
Saumyanayaki Temple, from southeast

SAUMYANAYAKI TEMPLE AND KALYANA MANDAPA

Northwest of the Kappe Chennigaraya stands the Saumyanayaki temple, a goddess shrine that is no earlier than the Vijayanagara period, being modified on several occasions. It is approached through a long, two-level open hall with reused Hoysala schist columns. The sanctuary and *mandapa* walls are crudely constructed from plain pillars and infill slabs. The brick and plaster tower above is of the Bhumija type, with tapering bands in the middle of each face, topped with a gilded, star-shaped finial. Its frontal projection is adorned with an ornate arch containing an image of Venugopala. The image in the sanctuary is installed within a gorgeous brass frame.

On axis with the Saumyanayaki, some 20 metres to the east, stands a lofty swing pavilion with four slender granite columns. Metal hooks for chains are affixed to its ceiling. Built up to the rear courtyard walls, immediately north of the Saumyanayaki, is an open structure containing a raised podium with four columns. This is typical of *kalyana mandapas* intended for marriage ceremonies associated with temple deities. Though no earlier than the Vijayanagara period, it incorporates Hoysala period columns and elephant balustrades.

OPPOSITE
Looking towards the swing pavilion and entrance *gopura*

BELOW
Viranarayana Temple, south *mandapa* wall

VIRANARAYANA TEMPLE

A few metres west of the Chennakeshava, and aligned with its main sanctuary, is the much smaller Viranarayana temple. It was probably erected by Ballala II towards the end of the 12th century, at the same time as his additions to the Chennakeshava.

The Viranarayana temple has a single sanctuary and vestibule opening into a square *mandapa* with four central columns, all elevated on a broad plinth, with access steps on the east. Its outer walls are divided into shallow projections, multiplied at the midpoints of the sanctuary and enclosed *mandapa*, where they are defined by pilasters and framed by colonettes. The projections have sculpted figures in pilastered niches

headed by Vesara temple towers crowned with *kuta* roofs, in shallow but sharp relief. Figures in the intervening surfaces are set beneath foliation, scrollwork or frames of crisply rendered, looped garlands. Other recesses have single pilasters carrying temple towers headed by extravagant looped garlands in shallow relief.

Though the Viranarayana figures are of high quality, the faces of most are damaged. Among the most interesting are naked Bhairava standing on his victim on the south face of the *mandapa*, and Bhima attacking Bhagadatta and his giant elephant on the north face, extending across the full width of the projection. Figures on the projections portray Narasimha (south), an enigmatic divinity with a trio of crowned heads holding conch and disc (west), and Shiva dancing on a crawling naked dwarf (north). A finely detailed *makara* spout emerges from the north side of the sanctuary. Like the Chennakeshava and Kappe Chennigaraya, there is no tower.

Access to the temple interior is problematic, since the acting priest only comes at unpredictable times.

ABOVE
Viranarayana Temple, Bhima attacking Bhagadatta wall panel

OPPOSITE ABOVE
Andal Shrine, from southeast

OPPOSITE BELOW
Andal Shrine, Varaha wall panel

ANDAL SHRINE

Northwest of the Chennakeshava stands a shrine dedicated to the Tamil poetess-saint who became popular during the 16th-17th centuries when this building was erected. Its sanctuary and *mandapa* walls have been assembled with imagination from columns and sculpted panels brought from dilapidated Hoysala monuments elsewhere, like the Kedareshvara and Nagareshvara at Halebidu (*see pages 107-111*). Among

the latter are fine panels of Lakshminarayana with attendants waving fly-whisks, and Krishna playing the flute (south), and two corner blocks showing Varaha and Trivikrama (southwest), and dancing Bhairava and Kali (northwest). The *mandapa* has a brick and plaster parapet, and a small square tower crowned with a dome-like roof, instead of a tower over the sanctuary.

The sanctuary interior is approached through an open columned hall employing reused Hoysala supports. Even the doorway, with dancing Shiva on the lintel, has been brought from elsewhere. The temple is usually open in the mornings, when the goddess within attracts numerous devotees.

STORE AND NORTH COLONNADE

Tucked into the northwest corner of the walled courtyard is a long, low structure with massive plain walls, devoid of windows except for repurposed Hoysala screens, now used as a store. The two lines of columns inside are of the Vijayanagara era, if not later.

ABOVE North Colonnade

BELOW Stepped Tank

The nearby colonnade running almost the full length of the north courtyard walls provides welcome shade during the hottest part of the day. It also offers visitors an opportunity of inspecting the numerous carved panels, *naga* stones, memorial stones and inscribed slabs set into the walls. Among the finest pieces here is a long slab portraying the Saptamatrikas with Shiva and Ganesha.

STEPPED TANK

Located in its own low-walled enclosure in the northeast corner of the courtyard is a small, square stepped tank. This is identified with the Vasudeva *tirtha* mentioned in the inscription in the Chennakeshava temple listing Ballala II's contributions to the complex. The tank's enclosure is entered from the west through a small gate, with a doorway framed by slender colonettes, with Gajalakshmi on the lintel, and faceted half-columns at either side. After passing through the gateway, visitors descend down to the water, contained on three sides by steep stepped sides.

Small, west-facing shrines, now empty, occupy the two corners of the enclosure. Their doorways are flanked by tiny guardians, maidens and leaping *yalis*. Finely finished spires above are of the Bhumija variety, with eight tapering bands flanked by model towers, capped with *amalakas* and pot finials.

SHRINES SOUTH OF THE *GOPURA*, ELEPHANT GATE AND *VAHANA* PAVILION

A line of small shrines opening into a colonnade runs along the east courtyard wall between the *gopura* and elephant gate. Of recent construction, the shrines accommodate different deities, whose names are given over the doorways. That immediately south of the *gopura* is consecrated to Ramanuja, who is supposed to have met and influenced the Hoysala king Vishnuvardhana. The seated portrait of the philosopher-teacher is impressive for its noble simplicity.

Vahana Pavil on

The so-called elephant gate, through which animals could pass at festival times, is usually closed. While it employs Hoysala period columns for its inner and outer porticos, it is no earlier than the 16th century. A government school is built into the gate's outer face.

Reused Hoysala pieces are also incorporated into the kitchen, stores and other structures built up to the south courtyard wall. Here too is a pavilion with a ground level court surrounded on three sides by colonnaded platforms, once used for displaying metal statues of the Alvars, the popular poet-saints of Tamil origin. The pavilion today serves as a store for splendid, gilded *vahanas* of Hanuman and Garuda, and peacock, elephant and leaping horse. These are all used for conveying deities during temple festivals.

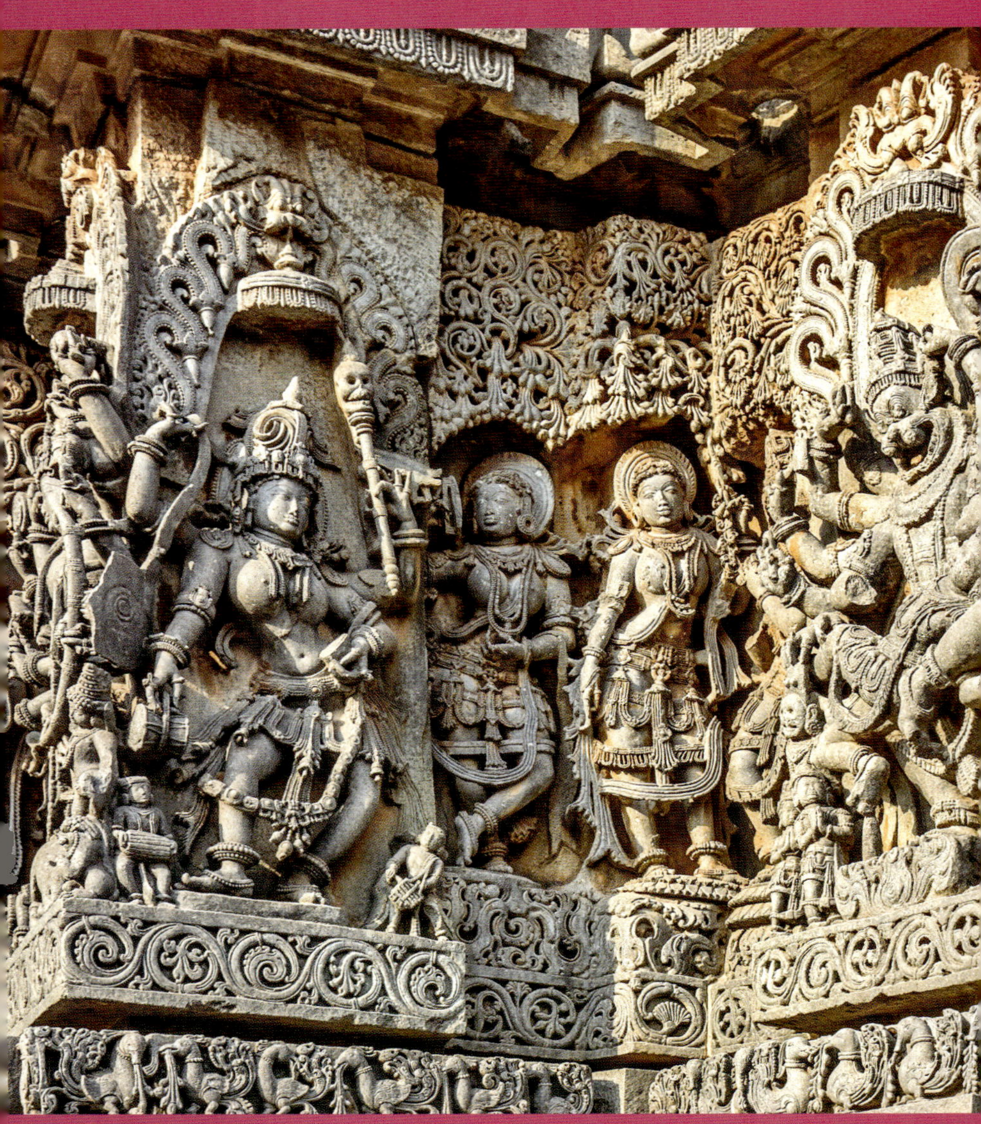

Hoysaleshvara Temple, wall sculptures

HALEBIDU

Apart from the Hoysaleshvara temple, which draws crowds of visitors each day, almost nothing survives at Halebidu to suggest that in the 12th and 13th centuries this was Dvarasamudra, capital of the Hoysala kingdom. After the plunder of the city by the troops of the Delhi sultans at the beginning of the 14th century and its subsequent abandonment by the Hoysalas, the place came to be known as the Old Settlement (Halebidu), the name it bears today.

THE SITE

A vast tank stretches eastward from the Hoysaleshvara temple, after which Dvarasamudra derives its name ("Ocean at the Gates"). Sadly, this has lacked water for a number of years, giving little idea of the elaborate hydraulic works that once supplied the city. As for the ramparts that protected the capital, fanning out from the tank in a half circle more than 2 kilometres across, these are now severely eroded and overgrown. Isolated portions with huge, roughly shaped granite boulders set into steep earthen embankments can be made out at the eastern edge of the fenced compound of the Hoysaleshvara, and beside the roads leading west towards Belur, south towards Hulikere, and north out of Halebidu town. There is, however, no trace of the gateways in these ramparts through which these roads once passed.

Beneath the eastern flank of the low hill of Bennegudda that rises in the middle of the site is a zone marked on old maps as a palace area, where the Hoysala monarchs are supposed to have resided and ruled. However, nothing can be made out here today, other than stone blocks of a retaining wall, several low earthen mounds, and tilled fields dotted with partly buried stone blocks. While there is no broken pottery on the surface of the ground to indicate past occupation, future excavations may yet reveal buried remains.

Surviving portion of the city's ramparts

Other religious monuments dotted around the site, and even beyond the city walls, give an idea of Dvarasamudra's original extent. They include a Jain complex with a trio of *basadis*, the restored Kedareshvara temple, and the ruinous Nagareshvara complex. Other small, mostly rebuilt shrines include those on the fringe of Halebidu town to the north of the Hoysaleshvara.

(*These features are all located on the map of Halebidu inside the rear jacket.*)

HOYSALESHVARA TEMPLE

Visitors arriving from tour buses, cars and rickshaws reach the temple from a gate on the north (open dawn to dusk) along a path lined with shrubbery. In Hoysala times this may have been the public approach to the monument, in contrast to that from the south, the direction of the palace zone, reserved for the king and court.

Historical Context Considering its ambitious scale, double sanctuaries and profusion of carvings, it is surprising to discover that the Hoysaleshvara lacks clear information about its foundation. This is in striking contrast to the Chennakeshava at Belur, which is provided with a lengthy inscription specifying Vishnuvardhana as the royal patron, the date of its construction, and its original dedication. While there can be little doubt that the Hoysaleshvara belongs to the reign of Vishnuvardhana, this king evidently felt no need to proclaim his sponsorship of this grandly conceived temple. Erected in the heart of his capital, it is provided with twin *linga* sanctuaries consecrated to Vishnuvardhana as Hoysaleshvara and his principal queen Shantaladevi as Shantaleshvara.

See photograph on pages 20-21

It is sometimes believed that a subordinate of Vishnuvardhana was solely responsible for its construction. An inscribed slab dated 1121 found at Ghattadahalli, a village 5 kilometres east of Halebidu, mentions a merchant-officer named Ketamalla building a temple at Dvarasamudra, naming it Hoysaleshvara after his royal overlord. (The slab is now in the Archaeological Museum at Halebidu, but the Kannada letters engraved on its surface have altogether worn away.) Ketamalla's text repeats the dynastic history of the Hoysalas and the praises of Vishnuvardhana given in the Belur inscription. It is possible that Ketamalla acted as supervisor of the Halebidu temple, which was to be the largest of all Hoysala building projects. As a wealthy trader and businessman, Ketamalla may also have financed the entire cost, which would have been considerable. Another inscription, found over the temple's south entrance, mentions that its lintel was fashioned for the master architect of Narasimha I, perhaps soon after this ruler ascended the Hoysala throne in 1142.

Layout The Hoysaleshvara is of the *dvikuta* type, with two east-facing *linga* sanctuaries identified with Vishnuvardhana (south) and Shantaladevi (north). Each sanctuary is preceded by a vestibule opening into a *mandapa* with four central columns. The front (eastern) portions of the two *mandapas* are treated as porches with balcony seating, originally

FOLLOWING PAGES
Hoysaleshvara Temple, from south. See also photograph on pages 20-21

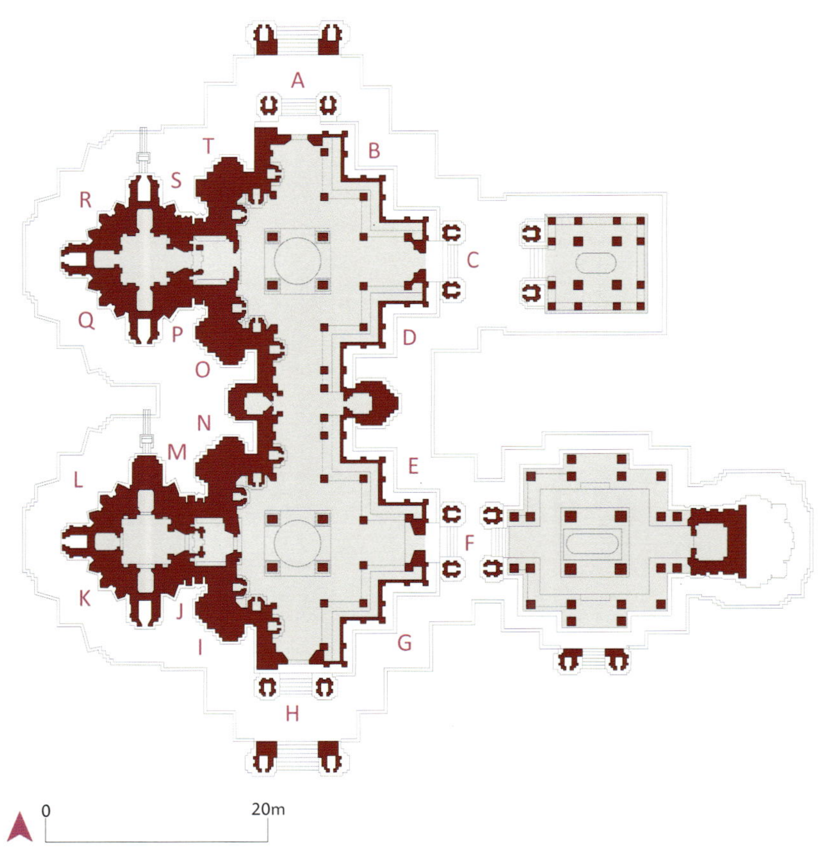
A
B
C
D
E
F
G
H
I
J
K
L
M
N
O
P
Q
R
S
T
0
20m

partly open, but later closed off with perforated stone screens. A passageway links the *mandapas*, with entrances on the north and the south (at A and H); two more entrances on the east (at C and F) give access to free-standing, open Nandi pavilions. (*See the plan opposite for the letters marking these and other locations.*) The *mandapas* employ the square as a basic unit of measure, with additional squares to create staggered plans. The same is true of the southern Nandi pavilion. In contrast, the *linga* sanctuaries are each laid out on 16-sided stellate plans, partly obscured by the adjoining vestibules and the small square subshrines protruding on three sides. Additional subshrines, accessible only from the temple interior, project outwards from the east and west midpoints of the passageway linking the two *mandapas*. (The walls of the subshrine on the east have been reconstructed.)

A platform, averaging 3 metres wide, 1.6 metres above the ground, runs continually around the two *mandapas*, *linga* sanctuaries and Nandi pavilions, perfectly echoing their complicated layouts. At its greatest extent, this measures more than 62 metres north-south and 68 metres east-west. The sides of the plinth are relieved by deeply cut mouldings, devoid of decoration. They are interrupted on the north and south, as well as twice on the east, by access steps flanked by model shrines with stunted Vesara towers with *kuta* roofs. Similar subshrines are positioned either side of the steps that climb from the plinth to the interiors of the *mandapas* and Nandi pavilions.

Exterior The walls of the *mandapas*, including their open porch portions, and the walls of both *linga* sanctuaries are raised on a basement that runs continuously around the temple, interrupted only by the four entrances. The more than 2-metre high basement is composed of eight friezes separated by deep incisions. The bottom five portray lines of high relief elephants, many with riders, proceeding towards the corners; similarly treated *yalis* with savage heads and curling tails, occasionally fighting; scrolling, leafy creeper in flat relief incorporating tiny figures; parades of horses, often with riders, in the company of foot soldiers and other martial figures and musicians; and a repeat of the scrolling creeper. The sixth course presents scenes from the *Bhagavata Purana*, *Mahabharata* and *Ramayana*. (*A selection of these is described in Appendix 1 on page 91.*) The topmost two courses show *makaras* with fantastic tails and diminutive riders, separated by looped garlands hanging from *kirtimukhas*; and *hamsas*

OPPOSITE
Hoysaleshvara Temple, plan

with elaborate tails. Visitors will appreciate the precision and inventiveness of these compositions, in which realistic elephants, horses and figures contrast with imaginary *yalis*, *makaras* and *hamsas*, and stylised creepers.

Porches marking the eastern halves of the two *mandapas* are provided with additional friezes. They show projecting panels filled with cut-out dancers and musicians in foliation, alternating with recesses with seated *yakshas*; and lines of tiny pyramidal temple towers of the Bhumija type. Pilasters framing warriors, musicians and seductive maidens adorn the angled backrest of the balcony seating above.

Porch columns with part-circular or occasional faceted shafts, and double capitals, carry the overhanging eave, its underside fashioned as ribs and rafters in imitation of timber construction. The corners of the eave terminate in cylindrical blocks of uncertain purpose, unlike the blocks projecting from the column capitals, which were clearly intended for angled brackets. Only at the east entrance to the king's sanctuary (F) are such brackets preserved, fashioned as female dancers, as at Belur. Stone screens with diagonal square perforations are somewhat crudely inserted between the peripheral columns, perhaps at the order of Narasimha I. (The two Mughal styled screens on face E are inappropriate, modern replacements.)

Panels with carved figures completely cover the rear walls of the *mandapa*, together with the indented buttress-like projections at the southwest and northwest corners. They continue on the projections at the midpoints between the two *mandapas*, as well as on the side walls of the vestibules and angled facets of the sanctuary walls. An astonishing array of gods, goddesses and attendants is seen here, the figures shown standing or seated on blocks adorned with creeper motif. (*The most interesting wall panels are described in Appendix 2 on page 95.*) Measuring almost 1 metre high, the figures are posed beneath foliage with naturalistic branches and leafy fronds, stylised scrollwork or looped garlands. The overall effect is that of an uninterrupted sculpted surface, with figures even carved onto the adjacent faces of corner blocks. The images on the king's sanctuary are for the most part superior in quality and more diverse in posture than those on the queen's sanctuary. The panels are overhung by an eave, with a shorter tier of walls above. These upper walls are enlivened with shallow pilasters, some carrying tiny temple towers or framing seated *yakshas* and other figures. They are sheltered by the main eave that runs around the whole building.

OPPOSITE
Basement friezes
See also photograph on page 28

HALEBIDU

Subshrines protruding from three sides of each of the *linga* sanctuaries rise on the six lower basement friezes of the walls at either side. Above these is a line of temple towers of different designs, as well as a meandering scroll inhabited by diminutive maidens, deities and warriors. The subshrines each have two superimposed chambers, with doorways flanked by tiny guardians between square and faceted colonettes carrying miniature eaves. Though now empty, the chambers have side walls with carvings, mostly of seated celestial couples. The upper chambers have miniature Bhumija towers punctuating the corners, as well as Vesara towers with *kuta* roofs extending up to the temple's main eave.

The *linga* sanctuaries of the Hoysaleshvara once functioned as royal chapels and would surely have been crowned with towers. That they have disappeared without a trace suggests that, like the tower recorded in the 19th-century photographs of Belur, they were of plastered brick on timber supports, and would have decayed after the temple ceased serving as a dynastic monument. If the towers resembled

East entrance to king's sanctuary

the superstructures of the subshrines below, as at Belur (*see page 56*), then these would have been of the Vesara type with *kuta* roofs. Given the lack of evidence, however, this can only be a supposition.

Entrances Subshrines beside the steps climbing to the *mandapa* entrances are supported on friezes of elephants and *yalis*. Their empty chambers have doorways sheltered by tiny eaves and capped with Vesara towers with small *kuta* roofs.

All four temple entrances were originally broad openings almost 4 metres across, which were only partly closed off when Narasimha I added slabs to carry intricately worked lintels. Almost human-size guardians placed either side of the two entrances leading to the king's sanctuary (F and H) appear in swaying, symmetrical poses. They hold drum, trident and skull- or flame-topped staffs, but one of their forearms is now missing. The jewellery, costumes, headdresses are rendered in immaculate detail, as are the foliate frames above headed by *kirtimukhas*. Smaller guardians brought from elsewhere are placed at the north entrance to the queen's sanctuary (A), but are absent at the east entrance (C). Lintels surmounting all four entrances depict dancing Shiva between diminutive Vishnu and Brahma. The figures are set within arches of scrollwork and looped garlands issuing from open-mouthed *makaras* with ornate tails and tiny riders, all rendered in the finest, filigree stonework.

Nandi Pavilions Free-standing Nandi pavilions are aligned with the *mandapa* entrances on axis with the temple's two *linga* sanctuaries. The pavilions are accessed from the west by steps flanked by Vesara subshrines identical to those beside the steps leading up to the temple *mandapas*, and linked to them by a continuous plinth. The smaller north pavilion has 16 part-circular columns, with additional square columns to support peripheral beams that were too long and began to crack; balcony seating is provided on four sides. The larger south pavilion, which employs similar columns, but has additional pairs of columns creating indented projections on four sides, also with balcony seating all around. Here, too, extra columns were later inserted for structural reasons. The central four columns in each pavilion, which are larger and more ornate, frame a seated bull, ceremonially decked with garlands, clappers and bells on its head, neck

BENEATH AND FOLLOWING PAGES
Nandi pavilion in front of king's sanctuary

and body. The animal in the south pavilion is slightly larger and more extravagantly embellished, since it faces towards the king's sanctuary. The pavilion ceilings are divided into panels filled with lotuses as well as tiny figures; that over the Nandi in the south pavilion shows Shiva spearing Andhaka surrounded by drummers and flautists. Adjoining the back of this pavilion is a partly dismantled shrine, its vestibule occupied by an impressive icon of Surya holding lotuses in the two hands. The seven horses of the sun god's chariot are carved onto the pedestal; on each side is a consort aiming an arrow.

Interior The two *mandapas* of the temple are linked by a 4-metre wide aisle to achieve a continuous space, almost 50 metres from north to south. Light flooding in from broad openings on four sides and from gaps between the outer (east) columns would have brilliantly illuminated the interior, enlivening the wall and column surfaces with sharp shadows, especially in the mornings. Later doorway frames and screens created a much darker interior. Stepped platforms for balcony seating around the porch portions of the *mandapas* would have encouraged priests and devotees to gather here before and after daily rituals.

In front of each *linga* sanctuary are four magnificent columns with cubical bases embellished with carvings, and part-circular, lathe-turned shafts with polished gleaming surfaces, interrupted by incisions and bands of ornament. They stand on raised floor areas inscribed with circles, sometimes believed to define performance spaces. Columns set into the raised balcony seating on the *mandapa* peripheries are either circular, but more slender than those in the middle, or have intricately worked, multi-faceted or stellate shafts and capitals. Brackets fashioned as dancing maidens beneath cut-out foliage once angled out from the central columns in both *mandapas*, but only a few of these are preserved. The beams support octagon-to-square ceilings: that in front of the king's sanctuary

OPPOSITE *Mandapa* interior, north-south aisle

BELOW *Mandapa* ceiling

Mandapa interior, Sala attacking beasts

is divided into roundels with eight-armed dancing Shiva surrounded by the Dikpalas. A similar Dikpala ceiling is found immediately inside the eastern entrance to the queen's sanctuary (C). Ceilings elsewhere are divided into different shaped compartments filled with lotus blossoms.

See photograph on p. 24

Shrines set into the walls on either side of the vestibule doorways have pairs of pilasters framing chambers that accommodated Shaiva deities, but which are now empty. Colonettes, some cut out, carry fully modelled eaves and Vesara towers with *kuta* roofs in high relief. Panels beneath show Sala brandishing sword and shield combatting one or even two savage *yalis*. These are the only representations of the Sala legend to be seen anywhere in the temple. Circular colonettes and guardians flank the doorways to the larger shrines at the midpoints of the corridor linking the two *mandapas* (now closed off by wooden doors). Here, too, Vesara towers are employed.

See photograph on page 29

See photograph on page 22

Guardians equally magnificent to those at the outer entrances to the *mandapa* flank the vestibule doorway leading to the king's sanctuary, accompanied by smaller maidens bearing fly-whisks. The pediment above, like those of the outer entrances, is highly ornate and partly cut out. Dancing Shiva with smaller figures of Vishnu and Brahma are set between *makaras* with foliated tails, and framed by an arch of looped garlands; similar garlands "hang" from the lintel over the opening. The vestibule doorway to the queen's sanctuary is similar, but less elaborate. The *linga* within is noticeably smaller than that in the king's sanctuary, and no longer receives worship. Sanctuary doorways have ornate jambs with tiny pilasters of different designs set in bands with diminutive relief *yalis* and figures.

Appendix 1: Basement Narratives on the Hoysaleshvara Temple

A selection of the narratives on the sixth basement course of the temple is described here in a clockwise sequence, individual scenes being located by letters marking the different sectors of the plan (*see page 80*). Beginning to the left of the temple's north entrance, we find the churning of the cosmic ocean, with the long serpentine body of Vasuki being tugged by gods and demons (many now missing their heads) (B). Then follow Shiva and Parvati with Nandi, Ganesha and Brahma, attended by the Dikpalas riding their respective animal mounts: Indra on the elephant, Agni on the ram, Yama on the buffalo, Varuna on the *makara*, etc. (B). The next scenes of interest illustrate the *Bhagavata Purana* (E): youthful Krishna killing Putana and the crane demon; uprooting the two trees; looting butter from hanging pots; playing the flute in the company of singing cowherds and herdesses; lifting Govardhana; riding with Balarama in a chariot; and finally reaching the Yamuna river, depicted flowing across the panel from top to bottom.

Chariots with warriors shooting arrows through the air that follow illustrate various combats in the *Mahabharata* (G). Then comes the first depiction of the *Kiratarjuniya* (I): Arjuna leaving his brothers and Draupadi;

Basement narratives
TOP From the Krishna story

BOTTOM From the *Mahabharata*

TOP AND BOTTOM Basement narratives from the *Kiratarjuniya*

meeting Indra disguised as an ascetic in the forest, with the sages' wives pounding rice nearby; with Shiva, both of them shooting and killing the same boar; and then performing penance by standing on one leg (actually belonging to an earlier part of the story). Another *Mahabharata* scene portrays Bhima vigorously attacking his rival Bhagadatta mounted on the giant elephant Supratika (J). The torments of Prahlada, Vishnu's loyal devotee, portray the youth in the company of executioners, among writhing snakes, and between elephants that threaten to crush him, before meeting Hiranyakashipu, who is then slain by Narasimha (L).

Mahabharata episodes follow, notably that depicting Bhima killing Dushasana, drawing out the warrior's intestines so that Draupadi can dress her hair with them (N). An unidentified scene nearby shows parents slaying a child as a gruesome offering to Kali, followed by a selection of scenes from the *Ramayana* (N).

An unusually long block in the next sector of the basement is devoted to a second, more complete rendition of the *Kiratarjuniya* (O). Here Arjuna standing on one leg resists the allure of nearby maidens; Shiva and Arjuna together shoot a wild boar, and then fight each other, as witnessed by forest ascetics; finally Arjuna pays homage to Shiva who appears with Parvati to grant him the magic weapon. A more extensive treatment of the *Ramayana* follows (O): Rama and Lakshmana meeting the monkeys; Rama and Sita seeing the golden deer; Rama and Lakshmana receiving Hanuman and Sugriva; Sugriva and Vali fighting; Rama shooting an arrow through the seven palm trees to slay Vali; Sugriva being crowned; Rama giving his signet ring to Hanuman; and finally, Rama reunited with Sita.

The last narratives to be noticed on the temple basement are drawn from the *Mahabharata* (R). They begin with the formidable, labyrinthine formation of the Kaurava army, crowded with tiny figures. To one side Abhimanyu in a chariot aims arrows at Drona who defends the Kauravas, but then enters the labyrinth where he continues to fight, his body riddled by arrows, before dying. In the adjacent panel, Krishna relates the tragic news to Arjuna as the two bathe in a stepped pool filled with lotus stalks. Then come repeated depictions of Bhima slaying Dushasana, and fighting Bhagadatta's elephant.

Basement Narratives

TOP AND MIDDLE
From the *Ramayana*

BOTTOM
Labyrinth of the Kauravas in the *Mahabharata*

Appendix 2: Wall Panels on the Hoysaleshvara Temple

OPPOSITE
Krishna lifting Govardhana

Considering the Shaiva dedication of the monument, we note quite a few Vaishnava images, perhaps produced at workshops that had provided panels for the Belur temple. In addition to the many deities on the wall projections, there is an abundance of dancers, musicians and attendants in the intermediate recesses, many of them of outstanding artistic quality. As with the basement narratives, the wall panels noticed here are located by letters (*see page 80*).

Beginning immediately to the left of the temple's south entrance (H) is a dancing Ganesha depicted with fleshy head, trunk, stomach and limbs, one foot placed firmly on the rat. Then come triple-headed Brahma riding on a *hamsa*, with a watery branch in its beak; Arjuna winning the hand of Draupadi by aiming an arrow at a fish target atop a column, while turning his head away to observe the target's reflection in a basin of water below; and seated Sarasvati strumming a string of the *vina*, in ecstasy from the divine music that she is playing (I). Two energetic scenes follow (J): Krishna lifting Govardhana, witnessed by lines of cows, herdsmen and *gopis*; and Shiva jubilantly dancing in the skin of the elephant demon he has just slain, the animal's head, trunk and torso clearly visible beneath, accompanied by miniature drummers and seated Nandi.

Equally dynamic are the portrayals of boar-headed Varaha striding purposefully upon the body of the demon who had trapped Bhudevi, affectionately nuzzling the goddess whom he lifts up on one arm (K); two renditions of Shiva dancing on the dwarf (K and L); Durga spearing Mahisha (K); Trivikrama with one leg kicked high to encompass the ocean shown with wavy watery lines (M); and Garuda clutching a cobra (M). Three adjacent panels in the following sector (N) depict Vishnu on flying Garuda rescuing Gajendra from a lotus pond in which the animal had become trapped; Indra and his consort Shachi riding on the great elephant Airavata; and Vishnu with Lakshmi being transported through the air by Garuda with outstretched wings. These last two panels illustrate the legend of Vishnu stealing the celestial Parijata tree that belonged to Indra's consort, leading to the battle between the two gods. This sequence ends with standing Vishnu, seemingly an unexpected choice for the buttress-like projection marking the midpoint between the two *linga* sanctuaries (between N and O).

ABOVE
Vishnu and Lakshmi on Garuda approaching Indra and Shachi on Airavata

OPPOSITE
Ravana shaking Kailasa

See photograph on page 102

Panels on the next sector of walls (P) begin with two violent figures: Narasimha disembowelling Hiranyakshipu; and dancing skeletal Kali. Naked Bhairava is repeated on two faces of a corner block here, while also appearing together with dancing Shiva in the following sequence (Q). One of the most celebrated compositions on the temple is that showing Ravana with multiple heads and arms shaking Kailasa, the trees and forests on the mountain populated with minute figures, animals and birds, and Shiva and Parvati seated unperturbed at the summit (S). In the adjacent panel, a magnificent, multi-armed Shiva, holding bow and arrows, skull-topped mace and slender trident, paces out the steps of his cosmic dance on a crawling, crowned demon with bulging eyes and tusks. The sequence of wall panels ends much as they began, with auspicious Ganesha, here shown twice, both seated and dancing (T).

OPPOSITE
Dancing Ganesha

LEFT
Arjuna shooting an arrow at the fish target

FOLLOWING PAGES
Vishnu and dancing goddess with musicians, and Shiva dancing

ARCHAEOLOGICAL MUSEUM AND BRAHMESHAVARA TEMPLE

After completing their tour of the Hoysaleshvara, visitors with more time at their disposal may wish to inspect the nearby Archaeological Museum (ticket office open 9:00 am to 5:00 pm). Numerous sculpted blocks, many of them damaged and of lesser quality than those on the temple itself, are on display in the open air. One of the better preserved shows Krishna lifting Govardhana mountain. Here, too, can be seen a selection of hero stones and inscribed slabs. Inside the museum there are additional panels, several engraved copper-plates, a massive iron vessel, and a small, sensitively modelled bronze statue of Adinatha. Visitors should not neglect the huge granite Tirthankara set up within a later stone frame outside the museum. Almost 4 metres high and lacking one of its lower arms, the naked figure is admirable for its slender proportions, refined simplicity and smooth modelling.

Immediately south of the Hoysaleshvara are the stone blocks defining the passageway of a large gate lined with mouldings, now much rebuilt. If, as is

ABOVE
Tirthankara outside the Archaeological Museum

LEFT
Ganesha on the south gate

supposed, the Hoysala palace was situated southwest of the temple, then the king and his retinue might have passed through this gate on their way to the temple's south entrance. A splendid Ganesha removed from some nearby location is placed here. The elephant head, tusks, sinuous trunk, corpulent pot-belly and folded legs are all smoothly modelled, in contrast with the crisp detail of the god's crown, the objects held in the rear hands, and the surrounding frame. Two broken blocks depicting the Sala legend are seen opposite, possibly removed from the original towers of the temple.

A memorial pillar with carved figures progressing around the bottom of its circular shaft stands near the temple's southwest corner. The inscription on its cubical base relates the tragic story of Kuvara Lakshma, a bodyguard of Ballala II, who killed himself after his royal master died.

ABOVE
Memorial pillar

BELOW
Brahmeshvara Temple

Landscaped gardens and orchards, doubtless altering the historical context of the Hoysaleshvara, occupy the fenced compound in which the temple stands. This is bordered on the east by ramparts, beneath which recent excavations have revealed the basements of three shrines of uncertain dedication and purpose facing towards the great

tank. Hidden by trees in the extreme southeast corner of the compound stands the Brahmeshvara temple, its collapsing stonework shored up by steel scaffolding. In spite of its dilapidation, the temple preserves a finely worked shrine doorway, as well as portions of the eight-tiered basement beneath the stellate angles of the sanctuary's outer walls. Among the better preserved narratives here are those on the south illustrating *Ramayana* episodes: the crowning of Sugriva; Rama giving his ring to Hanuman; monkeys travelling through the forest then arriving at the ocean; the battle between Rama and Ravana; and the final happy reunion of Rama and Sita.

JAIN *BASADIS*

Some 400 metres south of the Hoysaleshvara are three north-facing Jain monuments standing next to each other within a walled compound, just south of Bastihalli, a small settlement with traditional tile-roofed houses. The Jain compound is entered from the north through a gate with a columned portico aligned with the largest and earliest of the *basadis*, dedicated to Parshvanatha. A slab set up beside its entrance has an inscription attesting that it was erected in 1133 by Boppanna, son of Gangaraja, one of Vishnuvardhana's trusted ministers and generals. The text is surmounted by a Jina seated between attendants and elephants.

BELOW
Parshvanatha *basadi*, from northeast

See photograph on page 16

Parshvanatha *Basadi*
LEFT
Mandapa ceiling

RIGHT
Parshvanatha image

An open square pavilion, its steps flanked by elephant balustrades, precedes the Parshvanatha *basadi*. Its 12 interior circular columns are surrounded by 20 more slender supports. The pavilion leads to the main doorway of the *basadi*, flanked by faceted colonettes and columns, with a Jina on the lintel. The majestically scaled *mandapa* within has columns with polished, part-circular shafts relieved by delicately incised garlands and scrolls. The central four columns carry a ceiling with rotating octagonal courses with Dikpalas and Jinas carved onto the sides; the square panel above has a relief depiction of the Jain *naga* deity Dharanendra. From here visitors can view the colossal granite image of Parshvanatha installed within the sanctuary. The 4.5-metre high, cut-out naked saviour stands immobile in front of the sinuous coils of the cobra, its seven hoods fanning out protectively over the head.

The Parshvanatha *basadi* presents an austere exterior, its plain walls relieved only by slender pilasters. Basement mouldings at the sanctuary have projecting *makara* heads, while the parapet above has tiny *yakshis* and meditating Jinas, some set in ornate *kudus* headed by *kirtimukhas*. No tower seems to have been intended.

The easternmost of the three *basadis* was erected in 1196 during the reign of Ballala II, but later expanded. It is similar to the Parshvanatha, but less refined. The 7-metre high *dipastambha* standing in front is topped with a tiny pavilion housing seated Brahma, considered a protective deity in the Karnataka Jain tradition. The monument houses a huge, gleaming stone statue of Shantinatha, the Tirthankara to whom the *basadi* is consecrated. A collapsing, overgrown stepped tank nearby occupies the northeast corner of the compound.

The smaller, more crudely built Adinatha *basadi* in the middle of the complex dates from 1138. A finely carved image of Sarasvati has been placed in its *mandapa*.

KEDARESHVARA TEMPLE

Continuing for another 400 metres along the road running east from the Jain *basadis* visitors will reach the Kedareshvara temple, which stands in a fenced compound entered through a small gate. The temple was built in 1219 by Abhinava Ketaladevi, queen of Ballala II, and in the following year endowed by Narasimha II, the next ruler, in honour of his mother Padmaladevi. After the decline of the Hoysalas the monument fell into disrepair. It was then substantially rebuilt at the turn of the 20th century, when many of its carvings were removed and its collapsing tower demolished, leaving the flat-roofed building that is seen today.

ABOVE
Dipastambha in front of the Shantinatha *Basadi*

BELOW
Kedareshvara Temple, from northeast

Kedareshara Temple, basement narratives
ABOVE From the *Mahabharata*

RIGHT From the *Ramayana*

The Kedareshvara is a *trikuta* temple, having sanctuaries with stepped square plans on the north and south, and a third sanctuary with a stellate plan on the west, all opening into a columned *mandapa*. The basement beneath the walls of the *mandapa* and the three sanctuaries has a narrative course upon lines of elephants, horse-riders, creepers, *yalis*, *makaras* and *hamsas* (there are many replacement blocks). A scene worth seeking out from the *Mahabharata* shows Bhishma dying on a bed of arrows (south face of south sanctuary). *Ramayana* compositions occur on the west face of the south sanctuary, and the angles of the stellate shrine that follow. In clockwise sequence they depict: Ravana carrying Sita away; Rama and Lakshmana meeting Hanuman; Rama aiming an arrow through the seven palm trees; Vali and Sugriva fighting; monkeys building the causeway to Lanka, with the monkeys bringing rocks towards the flowing waters of the ocean; monkeys battling; the slaying of Ravana; and the crowning of Rama and Sita in the company of the monkeys. Then comes a charming but enigmatic scene of a fish pond with bathers and flying figures, followed by *Kiratarjuniya* episodes: Arjuna performing penance; shooting the wild boar; fighting Shiva who is disguised as a hunter; and finally prostrating himself before Shiva to receive the magic weapon. Further along there are *Mahabharata* battle scenes, some with fallen warriors, and even the labyrinth of the Kauravas in which Abhimanyu becomes trapped.

Though many wall panels of the Kedareshvara have been re-assembled haphazardly, several are equal in quality to those of the Hoysaleshvara. Proceeding clockwise from the south sanctuary, they include: Rama and Lakshmana standing beneath a tree; Shiva and Parvati riding majestic Nandi; naked Bhairava and Bhikshatana (two faces of a corner panel of the west sanctuary); Krishna dancing on Kaliya, the youthful god holding up the serpent's long tail; a grotesque dancing Kali; Krishna lifting up Govardhana; imposing Shiva dancing in the elephant skin (northwest corner of the *mandapa*); Arjuna shooting an arrow at the fish target; and Ravana shaking Kailasa (north sanctuary).

These and other panels occupy the lower tier of walls, separated by an eave from a shorter, upper tier of walls occupied by shallow pilasters and tiny temple towers. A second, similar overhang terminates the walls, but nothing now survives of the overgrown, partially collapsed

Kedareshvara Temple, wall panels
LEFT
Shiva and Parvati on Nandi

BELOW
Krishna dancing on Kaliya

Vesara tower over the stellate sanctuary visible in the 19th-century photographs. Towers of the same type, though on square layouts, may once have surmounted the other two shrines.

The *mandapa* interior of the Kedareshvara has columns with faceted stellate shafts as well as those with lathe-turned circular shafts. The latter carry an ornate, octagon-to-dome ceiling with a central pendant lotus bud. Wall niches are topped with temple-like towers, but are now empty, like all three sanctuaries.

Adventurous visitors with an interest in military architecture may wish to explore the overgrown ramparts in the vicinity of the Kedareshvara temple. About 100 metres southeast of the temple compound is a narrow, stone-lined passageway, around 11 metres long and 1.3 metres wide. This may have served as an escape route leading down to the Dvarasamudra tank.

ABOVE Passageway in the ramparts

BELOW Hulikere, Tank

HULIKERE

Returning from the Kedareshvara temple to the Jain *basadis*, visitors should take the road running south for about 1.5 kilometres, and then turn left (east) along a country road for another 1 kilometre in order to reach the small settlement of Hulikere. This is of interest for its remarkable square tank dating from the period of Narasimha I in about the middle of the 12th century. Steps on four sides descend from lines of model shrines topped with stunted Vesara towers with *kuta* roofs, like those beside the access steps of the Hoysaleshvara. A slab near the steps on the west side portrays a hero armed with bow and arrow fighting an opponent bearing a shield.

NAGARESHVARA COMPLEX

About 200 metres west of the Hoysaleshvara, immediately behind Hotel Mayura Shantala, is the extensive but greatly ruined Nagareshvara complex. Excavations here in the 1980s revealed the stone basements and rubble lower walls of three identical, east-facing temples, each with a trio of stellate sanctuaries, disposed in a north-south row. They are approached from a gate to the east, its broad passageway aligned with the central temple. While the walls of the *linga* sanctuaries and adjacent vestibules have altogether disappeared, the basements with tiers of carved friezes partly survive. Those of the southernmost temple are the best preserved. They show a full series of elephants, horse-riders, continuous creepers, narrative scenes, *makaras* and *hamsas*, all carved with utmost precision. *Ramayana* episodes prevail on the south face: the crowning of

Nagareshvara Temple, from north

Nagareshvara Temple, basement narratives from the *Ramayana*

Sugriva; Rama giving the ring to Hanuman; the monkeys searching for Sita; the monkeys trapped in the cave; the monkeys reaching the ocean; the monkeys carrying rocks in the act of building the causeway to Lanka; and Hanuman meeting Ravana, and then setting fire to Lanka.

TEMPLES IN HALEBIDU TOWN

Among the religious monuments to be seen in the northern part of Halebidu town is the recently restored Virabhadra temple. The outer walls of its sanctuary have panels of Brahma (south), Shiva (west) and

Narasimha (north), while the pyramidal Phamsana tower above has a frontal projection with a cut-out representation of Sala fighting the tiger, the only representation at Halebidu of the topic in such a location. Carvings set into the walls of the adjoining *mandapa* have been brought from other monuments, but the large image of Virabhadra armed with weapons installed in the sanctuary may be original.

Immediately north stands the Gudleshvara temple, rebuilt on a Hoysala plinth, but with its original porch intact. To the south is a deep square tank approached by two steep flights of steps. A segment of Halebidu's ramparts, with huge boulders set into earthen walls, can be seen a few metres east of the road in front, which here may have passed through one of the city's gateways.

The Ranganatha temple elsewhere in the town has an original Phamsana tower, but the remainder of the building, including its doorway and the gate in front, have been rebuilt entirely. The large Hoysala period image of Vishnu asleep on Ananta within has been brought from some other location, as have the carved slabs assembled outside.

Halebidu Town, Virabhadra Temple

Keshava Temple, from east

SOMANATHAPURA

KESHAVA TEMPLE

This outstanding example of late Hoysala architecture and art is located near to the Kaveri river in the southernmost part of Karnataka. Somanathapura is a tranquil village with traditional tile-roofed houses, most conveniently reached from Mysuru, 35 kilometres to the west, or at a slightly lesser distance from Srirangapattana on the Bengaluru-Mysuru highway. The Keshava temple here was associated with a Brahmin *agrahara* and formed part of a wider sacred geography that extended up to the Kaveri, consisting of religious structures and subsidiary shrines of both Vaishnava and Shaiva affiliation. The temple stood within a rectangular enclosure defined by earthen walls measuring 635 metres by 385 metres. The *agrahara* and enclosure have now disappeared, together with the ceremonial pathway that once led to the Panchalingeshvara temple some 300 metres to the east.

Dipastambha and entrance gate

The Keshava temple is reached at the end of a walkway that traverses pleasant lawns within a fenced compound (ticket office open 8:30 am to 5:30 pm). Among the sculpted panels displayed here is one of Yoganarayana, the meditating form of Vishnu. In front of the entrance gate to the temple is a 10-metre high, granite *dipastambha* with a slender, part-16-sided shaft. This is crowned with a double capital, but is now missing its topmost metal candelabra for oil lamps.

Gate and Courtyard

The outer appearance of the reconstructed entrance to the temple gives little indication of the perfectly preserved monument within. The gate has a spacious, *mandapa*-like interior with finely worked schist columns. Unpolished, part-circular shafts and double capitals carry octagonal and square panelled ceilings filled with lotuses. Set up to the left inside the gate is a 2.8-metre high slab with an inscription of 91 lines in Old Kannada characters, in both Sanskrit and Kannada languages. This gives information about the patron of the temple, the date of its construction equivalent to 1268, and the provisions made for the worship of its three deities and the livelihood of its employees. The text continues with an account of the rise of the Hoysalas and their genealogy down to Narasimha III. It then relates that when this king was seated in the council chamber in his capital Dvarasamudra (Halebidu), the commander Somanatha Dandanayaka requested funds to erect a Vaishnava monument and *agrahara* at his estate on the Kaveri, named after him as Somanathapura. A second inscription below lists additional bequests by Narasimha III in 1281 to merchants and teachers, while other inscriptions on the side faces of the slab register grants in 1300 and 1326 to priests and officers by the later ruler Ballalla III. These grants include details of temple rituals and ceremonies, shedding light onto religious practice in Hoysala times. The part-circular panel above the inscriptions depicts Keshava, Janardhana and Venugopala, the different aspects of Vishnu installed in the temple's three sanctuaries, surmounted by an elaborate *kirtimukha*.

Inscribed slab inside entrance gate

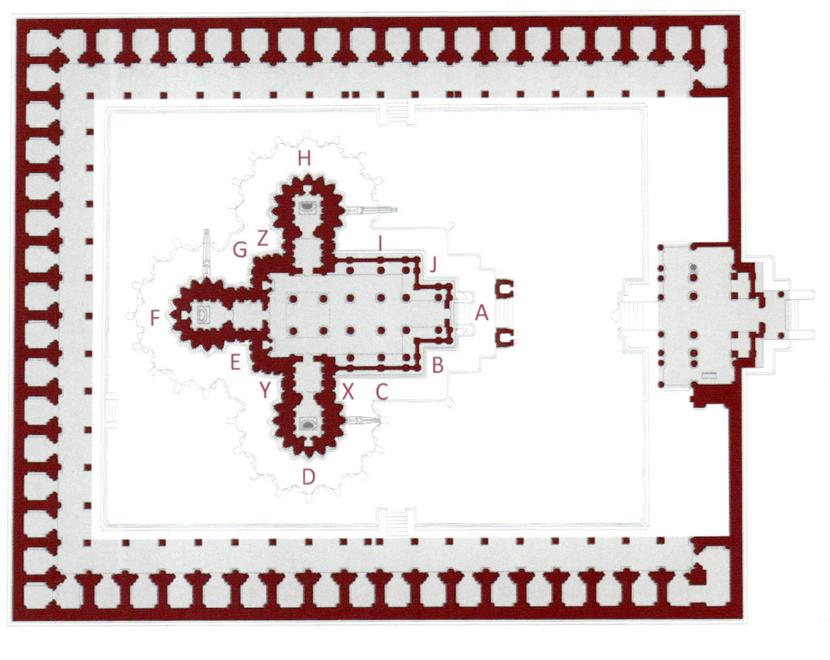
H
G
Z
I
J
F
A
E
B
Y
X
C
D
0
20m

ABOVE Sculpted elephant on temple plinth

OPPOSITE Temple plan

Steps descend from the gate to the paved courtyard in which the temple stands freely. Measuring 47 by 36 metres, the courtyard is defined by high granite walls, around which 56 small shrines are arranged on three sides, linked by a continuous colonnade. Shrines have plain doorways, with occasional friezes of relief model tower over the lintels. Damaged carvings are placed inside several of the shrines, as well as on the podium to the south of the gate, where the shrines were removed some time ago. Inscriptions in the colonnade record restorations to the main temple in 1497 and 1550 under local Vijayanagara governors.

Layout With its three fully preserved towered sanctuaries upon part-16-angled plans in stellate formation, the Keshava is to be regarded as one of the most perfectly designed specimens of a Hoysala *trikuta* temple. The sanctuaries are preceded by small vestibules that open from the north, west and south into a *mandapa* with four columns in the middle. The hall is extended eastward to create an overall rectangular interior of five by three bays, with an additional single bay serving as the entrance. The eastern half of the hall is treated as a porch, with balcony seating lit by perforated stone screens set between peripheral columns.

A plinth, 1.2 metres wide running around the temple imitates the building plan, including the angled facets of the three sanctuaries. Rising one metre above the pavement, the plinth has plain mouldings separated by deep recesses, with sculpted elephants on pedestals set up at many of the corners, especially those around the three sanctuaries. Subshrines, now missing their towers, flank a single flight of steps on the front (east) climbing from the pavement to the plinth.

Porch Exterior The porch extension of the temple's *mandapa* is entered through a doorway with sharply articulated but plain jambs and lintel fashioned from different coloured stone. It may be a later insertion. At either side are sculpted guardians standing within ornate frames; they each hold a conch and disc, but are missing both their forearms.

Basement friezes beside the temple doorway wrap around the north and south sides of the porch (faces I and J, and B and C). From

South sanctuary and *mandapa* porch, from southeast

bottom to top they depict elephants, many richly caparisoned and with riders, together with attendants; parades of cavalry with horses being ridden by armed soldiers accompanied by attendants; meandering creepers with foliated stems; and martial scenes with cavalry, foot soldiers and war chariots on the south, replaced on the north by battle

scenes from the *Mahabharata*. (***The latter are noticed in Appendix 1 on page 132.***). Then comes a line of single pilasters, in between which are tiny standing deities, mostly of Vishnu, as well as maidens and other figures. The pilasters support miniature pyramidal towers of both Bhumija and Vesara types, separated by rearing, curling-tailed *yalis*.

These last courses support the backrest of the porch balcony seating. This has a slightly angled surface divided by pairs of pilasters into panels with small compositions, many illustrating the story of Prahlada. To the right of the doorway (J), the youth is crushed by an elephant, beaten by a soldier, and tormented by flames, before pacifying his father Hiranyakashipu. To the left of the doorway (B), Prahlada meditates in the ocean, seemingly unharmed by piles of rock pelting down upon him, after which he meets Hiranyakashipu, and implores Narasimha for help. Fighting ensues, before Narasimha disembowels Hiranyakashipu. Amorous couples, in sexual union, fill many of the other backrest panels.

Square columns rising on the balcony seating within the porch present faceted shafts, capitals and heavy brackets. Stone screens in between the columns have diagonal square perforations separated by panels with decorative patterns. The columns carry a simple eave and a crudely restored parapet incorporating foliated *kudus* and *makaras*, as well as tiny deities and *yakshas*.

ABOVE
Torments of Prahlada, details of backrest

OPPOSITE
Mandapa porch basement mouldings, with backrest

FOLLOWING PAGES
South sanctuary, basement and wall panels

See photograph on pages 6-7

***Mandapa* and Sanctuary Exteriors** Basement mouldings running around the three sanctuaries and two western corners of the *mandapa* continue the lowest four friezes already noticed at the porch, but with minor variations. The elephants in the bottom frieze, some clad in military capes, proceed in different directions towards the corners. The parades of horse-riders in the second frieze depict in detail the trappings of the animals, as well as the swords, shields, daggers and other weapons wielded by riders and foot-soldiers, and the standards, parasols and musical instruments borne by attendants. Many horses are shown prancing, while others trample prone figures; camels occasionally appear (F). The creeper motif in the third frieze terminates in ferocious *kirtimukhas* at the corners of the sanctuary walls (D, F and H). The fourth frieze depicts legendary episodes. (*See Appendix 1 on page 132.*) The topmost two friezes show *makaras* with upturned snouts and *hamsas*, both with fanciful tails. Undecorated stone spouts protruding from the bottom friezes on the three sanctuaries continue as grooves across the surrounding plinth.

Pairs of slender pilasters frame the projections on the rear *mandapa* walls and angles of the sanctuary walls. The pilasters rise to the full height of the walls and appear to carry the overhanging eave running around the temple, here treated ornately with a frieze of pendant buds. Pairs of lower, secondary pilasters are partly obscured by 60-centimetre high, sculpted gods and goddesses. (*See Appendix 2 on page 135.*) Together with female attendants in the intervening recesses, these celestial figures stand beneath bunches of leafy foliation or frames of looped garlands; many have the artists' names engraved on the blocks beneath. The figures are topped by an intermediate eave, above which is an upper, shorter tier of walls. These have pairs of complex pilasters supporting high relief, stellate shrine towers of both the Vesara and Bhumija variety, with tiny vase-like pinnacles surmounted by *kirtimukhas* set in fanciful scrollwork.

The angles of the three sanctuaries are carried upwards into the four diminishing tiers of the Vesara styled towers that rise above. The density of ornament here makes it almost impossible to distinguish individual elements. The towers are composed of diminishing series of short walls with shallow pilasters framing tiny seated *yakshas*, many playing musical instruments. The pilasters carry double sets of eaves and blocks with foliated *kudus*. Other motifs represent scrolls, jewelled bands and musicians, dancers and *makaras*. The crowning roofs exhibit curved,

Sanctuary tower detail

fluted profiles that culminate in pot finials. Prominent projections with vault-like roofs protrude inwards from the towers, provided with frontal arches. The arches on the north and south contain images of dancing Vishnu surrounded by cut-out looped garlands and tufts of foliation headed by *kirtimukhas*. (These imitate dancing Shiva icons often found in these locations on Shaiva monuments.) The arch on the projection of the west tower is empty.

See photographs on page 3

ABOVE
Mandapa interior

OPPOSITE
Janardhana image in north sanctuary

Interior After the visual exuberance of the temple's sunlit exterior, the interior is dimly lit and sombre. Raised balconies with peripheral columns connect the entrance porch to the vestibules of the north and south sanctuaries. Columns are of the circular, lathe-turned variety with multiple incisions, but of substantial proportions, especially the four columns on the slightly raised square floor area of the bay in front of the three sanctuaries. These have deities carved onto their cubical bases, and projecting blocks on their lower capitals as if to take angled bracket figures. Part-faceted shafts and capitals distinguish the pair of columns marking the transition from the open to the closed parts of the *mandapa*.

Supported on beams with lotus motifs on their undersides and *yali* brackets, are 16 ceilings with a variety of designs that showcase the virtuoso skills of the Hoysala stoneworkers. The ceiling over the first bay on entering the interior comprises an octagon and concentric rings, while that over the bay in front of the sanctuaries employs 32 cut-out, radiating ribs. Other ceilings with similar ribs have octagonal, multi-lobed or 12-spoked frames, all with central pendant lotuses. Four ceilings in the side bays are of interest for their cut-out looped bands arranged in continuous, interweaving formations around a central lotus. All the ceilings incorporate diminutive celestials as well as musicians and other figures.

Jambs with delicately rendered pilasters with small guardians beneath frame the doorways to the three vestibules. Lintel blocks above depict the deities enshrined within: Keshava (west), Janardhana (north) and Venugopala (south). Subshrines headed by relief Vesara towers beside the west vestibule doorway are now empty. Two of the three sanctuaries preserve magnificent icons elevated on moulded plinths. These almost human-size, three-dimensional figures depict Vishnu as Janardhana holding lotus, conch, disc and mace standing within a frame of looped garlands issuing from *makaras* headed by a *kirtimukha* (north), and Krishna as Venugopala playing the flute beneath an intricate tree canopy, with herds of enraptured cows and their keepers at either side (south). The icon in the west sanctuary is a later replacement.

See photograph on page 31

Mandapa ceilings

Appendix 1: Basement Narratives on the Keshava Temple

The scenes on the fourth tier of the basement run in a clockwise sequence around the three sanctuaries and rear corners of the *mandapa* onto the north face of the porch. They begin with episodes from the *Ramayana* at "X"; *see plan on page 118*). Here, Dasharatha is seated in his palace surrounded by courtiers, soldiers and musicians, followed by battle episodes. The scenes around the south sanctuary (D) depict the king with sages and his three queens; the king's sacrifice in order to gain children; the three queens with four children on their laps; and the infants rocked in cradles, crawling on all fours, and then receiving martial lessons. Then come scenes of Rama killing Tataka, and defeating Maricha, whom he thrusts into the ocean; breaking Shiva's bow; and marrying Sita. Then follow the exile in the forest: Rama, Lakshmana and Sita riding in a chariot arriving at a river; Lakshmana disfiguring Surpanakha; Rama shooting the golden deer; and Ravana abducting Sita and slaying Jatayu, who falls to the ground. The story concludes with Rama and Lakshmana meeting Sugriva and Hanuman, and the monkeys arriving at the ocean, inhabited by fish and tortoises.

Having now reached "Y", where Vishnu is shown asleep on Ananta, the visitors will be able to follow the *Bhagavata Purana*, which runs in a continuous series from the southwest to the northwest corners of the *mandapa*, all around the west sanctuary (E to G). Vasudeva carries

TOP AND BOTTOM
Basement narratives from the *Ramayana*

the baby Krishna from prison, and crosses the Yamuna river to safety; Krishna is rocked in a swing, is suckled by matrons, and slays the ogress Putana by sucking at her breast, before looting the butter hanging in pots. As a youth, Krishna watches over the cows before arriving with his fellow herdsmen at the Yamuna, beyond which is dense forest populated by animals. Krishna then liberates the two brothers trapped in a tree, and defeats various demons, including the long-bodied snake Vasuki, before holding aloft Govardhana. After playing the flute, Krishna crosses the Yamuna, where he reaches the palace of Kamsa, whom he slays, before celebrating his triumph.

At this point visitors will have arrived at "Z", which is where the *Mahabharata* begins, proceeding around the north sanctuary, and continuing onto the north wall of the *mandapa* porch (Z to I). The opening episodes show Yudhishthira in his palace; Bhima shaking the Kauravas off their perch on a tree; and the fights between the Pandava and Kaurava boys. Then come battle scenes, witnessed by Bhishma and Drona seated in a pavilion. The Pandavas then escape to the forest, where Bhima kills the demon Hidimba and marries his sister. A cradle hanging from a tree represents the birth of their son Ghatotkacha. Bhima drives a cart full of food before killing a gluttonous demon. The Pandavas proceed to Drupada's town where they stay in a potter's house, after which Arjuna aims at the fish target and wins Draupadi. Extended chariot battles follow. A great meeting is held at Hastinapura where Yudhishthira loses the game of dice to the Kauravas. Krishna advises the Pandavas, and then Arjuna burns the forest, forcing the wild animals to flee. After the fight between Bhima and Dushasana, come the preparations for war, with soldiers bearing swords and shields, together with lines of elephants and camels. The climax of the story is represented by the five victorious Pandavas seated in state beneath a canopy, in the last scene to the north of the *mandapa* doorway (J).

Basement narrative from the Krishna story

Appendix 2: Wall Panels on the Keshava Temple

OPPOSITE
Vishnu seated on Ananta, wall panel

Almost 200 figures are sculpted onto the stellate angles of the three sanctuaries and the rear corners of the *mandapa*. The greatest number represent Vishnu in his various *avataras* and emanations, holding in his four or six arms the conch and disc, as well as the mace and club and other attributes. Visitors may notice a fruit-like object held in the hands of some figures bearing an uncanny resemblance to an ear of corn (American maize), a crop unknown in India in Hoysala times. Its identification remains mysterious, as does its significance.

Among the more interesting images are the following, listed here in clockwise sequence, beginning at the south sanctuary (D): Vishnu seated on the coils of Ananta, beneath the cobra's seven hoods; dancing Ganesha; dancing Sarasvati playing the *vina*; a sensitively rendered Venugopala, with the god playing the flute attended by *gopis* and cows; Vishnu holding the thunderbolt, suggesting he should be identified with Indra; and Rama holding the bow and arrow. Then follow Yoganarayana, showing meditating Vishnu, the hands placed in the lap; an unidentified female figure, perhaps Lakshmi; and Brahma with triple bearded heads. The next three aspects of Vishnu all have animal heads: the Matsya *avatara* shows the god with the snout and eyes of a fish; the Kurma *avatara* has a tortoise-like head; then comes an enigmatic, monkey-headed figure holding a peculiar, globular object. These are followed by Indra with his consort Shachi riding on the elephant Airavata, and Garuda flying through the air, bearing diminutive Vishnu and Lakshmi on his left arm. These two panels refer to the legend of Vishnu stealing Shachi's celestial Parijata tree. The last panel in this sequence depicts Narasimha seated with Lakshmi.

Wall panels elsewhere on the temple, especially those of Vishnu, are more standardised. Even so, those on the west sanctuary (F) are distinguished by figures with more satisfactory proportions and fully rounded bodies and limbs. Among the more unusual images on the angles of the north sanctuary (H) are those of dancing Sarasvati holding a *vina* and small book; Manmatha bearing the characteristic sugarcane bow; and Vishnu seated peacefully with Lakshmi. Here, too, is a striking icon of Vishnu as Kalki, armed with sword and rectangular shield; and a slightly damaged but vigorous portrayal of Durga, one leg thrusted firmly onto Mahisha, the bull she has just slaughtered. The signature of Mallitamma, the celebrated Hoysala artist, is engraved beneath these last panels.

Wall panels
ABOVE Standing Vishnu

RIGHT Dancing Sarasvati

Wall panels

ABOVE

Kalki

LEFT

Enigmatic figure

PANCHALINGESHVARA AND MONDUSALE TEMPLES

Within Somanathapura village, about 100 metres east of the Keshava temple, stands a small pavilion with four columns, now missing its roof. This was probably used at festival times for displaying processional images coming from the temple's shrines.

The ruinous, overgrown Panchalingeshvara temple stands outside the village, beside the road leading to T. Narasipura. Of its original five, east-facing *linga* shrines, only three survive to any extent. In contrast to the Keshava sanctuaries, these are built of greyish granite and are devoid of carvings. Eaves and parapets surmount plain walls with shallow pilasters, repeated in the two diminishing storeys of the Dravida-style towers with *kuta* roofs above. A long *mandapa* with rows of part-circular columns once linked the five shrines, but this has partly collapsed.

At the southern end of the Panchalingeshvara is an inscribed slab similar to that inside the entrance gate of the Keshava temple, and bearing the same date of 1268. This states that the temple was built

Panchalingeshvara Temple
BELOW
Towered *linga* shrines from southwest

OPPOSITE ABOVE
Top panel from inscribed slab

as a memorial for Somanatha Dandanayaka's family, two of the *lingas* being dedicated to his father and mother, and a third one bearing his own name. The part-circular panel above the text frames a male figure, probably the patron himself, worshipping a *linga* on a high pedestal, accompanied by a priest and two Nandis.

Among the overgrown, deteriorating Hoysala structures near the bank of the Kaveri, west of the Keshava, stands the Mondusale temple. The walls of its stellate, towered sanctuary lack carvings, but show a variety of model towers in shallow relief. Four part-circular columns survive inside the *mandapa*, but the frontal porch is now in danger of collapse.

BELOW
Mondusale Temple, from southwest

LEGENDARY NARRATIVES

Srikara Dattatreya

Here we summarise some of the legendary narratives presented so vividly on the basements and walls at Belur, Halebidu and Somanathapura, drawing attention to the most frequently depicted episodes.

Ramayana This popular epic relates the life of Rama, prince of Ayodhya, and embodiment of righteous rule. Rama is born along with his three brothers to Dasharatha, king of Ayodhya, and his three queens. From an early age, Rama exhibits outstanding martial abilities, especially when he repels the demons who interrupt the ritual observances of the sage Vishvamitra. Rama wins the hand of the princess Sita in marriage by stringing the great bow of Shiva.

Rama is named as the next king of Ayodhya, but falls victim to the jealousy of a stepmother who convinces Dasharatha to name her own son to succeed to the throne, and to banish Rama. In obedience to his father's wishes, Rama leaves the palace accompanied by Sita and his devoted brother Lakshmana. Wandering through the forests they encounter reclusive sages as well as various demons, including Surpanakha, sister of Ravana, king of the island Lanka. Rama repels her amorous advances, cuts off her nose, and Ravana takes vengeance. He sends a golden deer to distract Rama and Lakshmana, and then appears as a mendicant before Sita who had been left alone in a hermitage. He abducts Sita in his aerial chariot, but is intercepted by the vulture Jatayu, who falls fatally wounded to the ground, telling Rama and Lakshmana what has happened.

Wandering in search of Sita, Rama and Lakshmana come to the kingdom of Kishkindha, where they encounter the *vanaras*, the monkey people. They help the rightful monkey king Sugriva to win his throne back from his brother Vali, who had usurped him. Rama shoots an arrow through a line of seven palm trees and kills Vali. After Sugriva is crowned, he offers to help Rama find Sita, enlisting his monkey troops under their valiant general Hanuman who then sets off in search of Sita. Hanuman arrives in Lanka where he meets Ravana and discovers Sita confined in the palace. Preparations are then made to rescue Sita. The monkeys carry boulders to build a causeway to Lanka, and in the ensuing battle Rama and Ravana approach each other in war chariots surrounded by flying arrows. Ravana is killed, Sita delivered to safety, and Rama and Sita blissfully reunited. After an exile of 14 years Rama returns to Ayodhya where he is tumultuously welcomed and crowned.

Mahabharata This great epic relates the struggles of the five Pandava brothers, Yudhishthira, Arjuna, Bhima, Nakula, and Sahadeva, to regain the throne of Hastinapura that rightfully belonged to them, from their cousins, the Kauravas.

Pandu, the father of the Pandavas, was the ruling king of Hastinapura. Even before the Pandavas were born, he renounced his kingship, to live the life of a recluse in the forest along with his two wives, Kunti and Madri. It was there that the Pandavas were born. After the deaths of Pandu and Madri, Kunti returns to Hastinapura with her five infant sons.

The kingdom was then being ruled by Pandu's blind half-brother, Dhritarashtra, the father of the hundred Kaurava brothers, under the guidance of his uncle, Bhishma. The Kauravas are unsettled by the coming of the Pandavas to Hastinapura, as Yudhishthira had the right to the throne, being the eldest son of the rightful king, Pandu. Rivalry between the cousins ensues at a young age. On one occasion, as young children, the Kauravas taunt Bhima, said to have had the strength of many elephants, and climb up a tree in the assumption that he could not reach them. But with his immense strength, Bhima shakes the tree and brings them tumbling down. The Pandavas and Kunti survive an attempt at assassination and flee to the forest to escape further plots of the Kauravas.

While living as mendicants in the forest, Bhima slays the demon Hidimba and marries his sister and fathers a son with her named Ghatotkacha. He also slays a gluttonous demon who was troubling the residents of a village, by enticing him with a cartload of food. The Pandavas attend a contest to win the hand in marriage of princess Draupadi of Panchala. Arjuna succeeds in shooting an arrow to hit a fish target suspended above by looking down at its reflection in a bowl of water placed below. Though he succeeds in claiming Draupadi as his wife, when the Pandavas reach home with her, Kunti instructs them to share anything that they might have brought amongst themselves. Thus Draupadi becomes the wife of all the five Pandavas.

The Pandavas then return to Hastinapura with Kunti and Draupadi and lay claim to the kingship. Dhritarashtra resolves to partition the kingdom and award one half of it to the Pandavas. Arjuna burns a forest with his skills in archery in order to build the settlement of Indraprastha, which then becomes their capital.

Yudhishthira and Duryodhana, the eldest Kaurava, play a game of dice in which Yudhishthira gambles all his wealth and kingdom away. He finally gambles away even Draupadi, who is disrobed and humiliated by the Kaurava Dushasana. Having lost everything, the Pandavas are banished to the forest for 12 years. They were then mandated to live incognito and spent a year at the court of king Virata. Arjuna grows particularly strong during this period and even acquires a powerful weapon from Shiva (as described in the *Kiratarjuniya*). Soon after, he retrieves a herd of Virata's cattle that was stolen by the Kauravas.

After their exile ends, the Pandavas return to Hastinapura but the Kauravas refuse to return their portion of the kingdom. Negotiations led by Krishna ultimately fail and a great war ensues and many heroic battles take place. Bhima struggles against Bhagadatta riding on his great elephant Supratika, who is eventually killed by Arjuna with an arrow. Abhimanyu, a son of Arjuna, enters a labyrinthine battle formation of the Kauravas where he eventually dies. Bhishma is pierced with so many arrows that they form a bed on which he collapses and eventually dies. Bhima wrestles and kills Dushasana, and then removes his entrails to give to Draupadi to dress her hair, thereby avenging her humiliation. After enormous bloodshed, the Pandavas emerge victorious and assume the throne of Hastinapura.

Kiratarjuniya This story forms a part of the *Mahabharata*. While in exile, Arjuna performs rigorous penance in order to gain a powerful weapon from Shiva to be used in the impending war against the Kauravas. The god Indra, fearing that Arjuna might acquire power beyond his stature, sends musicians and heavenly damsels to distract him from his ascetic observances. He himself appears in the guise of a sage to dissuade Arjuna from his resolve., but is unsuccessful.

In order to test Arjuna's commitment to his penance, Shiva himself appears as a *kirata*, or as a mountain-dwelling hunter. Shiva and Arjuna shoot and kill the same wild boar simultaneously and a dispute ensues over who should claim the carcass. They aim arrows at each other and then wrestle. After Arjuna concedes defeat he realizes that he was fighting Shiva himself and prostrates himself in front of the god and his consort Parvati. Impressed with Arjuna's resolve and skill, Shiva rewards him with the *pashupata* weapon.

Story of Krishna (Bhagavata Purana) It was prophesised that a child of his own sister, Devaki, would bring death to the wicked tyrant, Kamsa, king of Mathura. Hence, he imprisoned Devaki and her husband Vasudeva, and killed each child born to them. But when Krishna, their eighth boy-child, was born, Vasudeva resolved to save the baby by slipping past the guard and carrying the child to safety across the Yamuna river. There he exchanged Krishna with the infant child of a cowherd named Nanda. Vasudeva then returned to his prison, and Kamsa killed the baby assuming that it was Devaki's child.

Kamsa soon learns that Krishna is alive, and he dispatches demons of many forms to find and kill him. One such is the female Putana, who arrives at Nanda's doorstep with an offer to breastfeed the infants of the house, and thus to kill Krishna with her poisoned teats. But when she raises Krishna to her bosom, he sucks her dry, resulting in her death.

Krishna as a baby is pampered by the cowherds. When they realize that he is too fond of butter, pots containing it are suspended at a height; even so, Krishna manages to get hold of the pots. In an attempt to curb his antics, Krishna's mother ties him to a heavy wooden mortar used to thresh wheat. With his sheer strength, Krishna breaks the mortar and crawls away with it. The mortar gets stuck between two trees, which he uproots with his unnatural strength, thereby releasing two heavenly spirits who were cursed to remain as trees.

As Krishna grows up he kills more agents of Kamsa, such as the giant serpent and crane-demon. He also subdues a cobra named Kaliya living in the river Yamuna by dancing on its hood. True to his upbringing among the cowherds, Krishna is in love with his cattle. He plays a flute to the rapture of the animals, fellow cowherds and especially the *gopis*, the herdesses who fancy him.

On one occasion, Krishna convinces his cowherd brethren to stop worshipping the god Indra, and to revere the Govardhana hill, which was the source of pasture for their cattle. An angered Indra sends a deluge in retaliation. But with his supernatural strength, Krishna lifts up Govardhana to shelter the cowherds and their herds from the tumultuous rain.

Kamsa invites Krishna and his elder brother Balarama to a wrestling tournament in Mathura, intending to murder them during the journey there. If that, failed, he would ensure that one of his strong wrestlers would kill Krishna during the competition. But these designs all fail, and Krishna escapes unharmed to challenge and kill Kamsa, thereby bringing his wicked rule to an end. Devaki and Vasudeva, as well as Kamsa's own father and the rightful king Ugrasena, are then released from captivity. Krishna and Balarama decide to stay on in the royal household of Mathura.

In the later part of the story Krishna plays the role of advisor to the Pandavas in the *Mahabharata*, as he rules over the kingdom of Dvarka.

Story of Prahlada The evil king Hiranyakashipu had become master of the heavens of the gods, the earth of the humans, and the underworld of the demons, on account of a boon that he had gained from Brahma from his rigorous penance. According to the boon, Hiranyakashipu could not be killed by either animal or any conscious being, neither during the day nor the night, neither on earth nor in the air, neither inside nor outside a building, and not with any weapon. Hiranyakashipu declared himself all powerful, dictating that everyone acknowledge him as a god. But his own young son Prahlada, who was an ardent worshipper of Vishnu, rejected his father's order. For this insolence, Hiranyakashipu sentenced him to death. But Prahlada's devotion shielded him from all his father's attempts to have him killed. The blows from soldiers' weapons caused him no harm, nor did venomous snakebites and trampling elephants, the flames from a furious pyre, or even the boulders under which he was buried in the ocean depths.

Exasperated, Hiranyakashipu demanded from Prahlada where Vishnu resided. When he replied that his god was omnipresent, Hiranyakashipu attempts to break open a pillar of the palace, feigning to look for Vishnu's presence in it. But a vicious creature emerges from the pillar, with the head of a lion and body of a man, who is the god's Narasimha *avatara*. It wrestles with Hiranyakashipu, carrying him to the threshold of the palace (neither inside nor outside a building), and hoisting him on his lap (neither on earth nor in the air). There, at twilight (neither during the day nor the night), Narasimha savagely tears open Hiranyakashipu's stomach with his claws (not any weapon) and pulls out his entrails. On Hiranyakashipu's death, Prahlada assumes his father's throne as king.

GLOSSARY OF ARCHITECTURAL TERMS

agrahara, Brahmin settlement supported by grants of land or income

amalaka, circular, ribbed pinnacle

basadi, Jain shrine

basement, exterior mouldings beneath floor level within

bay, space between columns or pilasters

Bhumija, central Indian temple style characterised by a curving spire with tapering bands flanked by tiers of model shrines

bracket, support for a beam

buttress, support for a wall

capital, topmost part of a column

colonette, small column

corbel, horizontal projecting block

cornice, topmost mouldings of a basement or wall

dhvajastambha, flagpole

dipastambha, lamp-pole

double capital, capital with two parts, often circular below and square above

Dravida, south Indian temple style characterised by a pyramidal, multi-storeyed tower crowned with a *kuta* roof

dvikuta, temple with two sanctuaries

eave, wall overhang

gopura, south Indian towered gate

kalyana mandapa, marriage hall

kudu, horseshoe-shaped motif in a cornice or eave

kuta, square-to-dome roof

lintel, beam spanning an opening

mandala, geometric cosmic diagram regulating a temple plan

mandapa, columned hall

matha, rest-house or monastery

Nagara, north Indian temple style characterised by a tower with a curved profile incorporating tiers of model towers

pediment, a design over an opening or wall niche

Phamsana, Deccan temple style characterised by a pyramidal tower with deeply cut, horizontal mouldings

pilaster, slender pillar-like element forming part of the wall surface

plinth, base course of a building

pradakshina, rite of clockwise circumambulation

sanctuary, chamber accommodating a temple deity

stellate, star-shaped, usually with 16 angles in Hoysala sanctuaries

subshrine, model temple with diminutive tower

tirtha, water tank or pool; place of pilgrimage

trikuta, temple with three sanctuaries

Vesara, Karnataka variant of the Dravida temple style

GLOSSARY OF INDIAN NAMES

Abhimanyu, Pandava warrior in the *Mahabharata*, son of Arjuna

Abhinava Ketaladevi, queen of Ballala II

Adinatha, first of the 24 Jain Tirthankaras

Agni, god of fire; one of the Dikpalas, guardian of the Southeast

Alvars, Tamil poet-saints

Ananta, serpent which protects Vishnu

Andhaka, demon killed by Shiva

Arjuna, Pandava warrior, hero of the *Kiritarjuniya* story

avatara, incarnation of Vishnu

Bali, demon king who granted a boon to Vamana

Ballala II, Hoysala king, ruled 1173-1220

Ballala III, Hoysala king, ruled 1292-1343

Bhagadatta, Kaurava warrior who rode the mighty elephant Supratika

Bhagavata Purana, story of Krishna

Bhairava, fierce form of Shiva

Bhikshatana, Shiva as a wandering ascetic

Bhima, Pandava warrior in the *Mahabharata*

Bhishma, Kaurava warrior in the *Mahabharata*

Bhu, Bhudevi, earth goddess; consort of Vishnu

Bhutanatha, name of Shiva

Boppanna, patron of Jain monuments under Vishnuvardhana

Brahma, four-headed creator god

Brahmeshvara, name of Shiva

Bukka, Vijayanagara king, ruled 1356-77

Chalukyas, 10th-12th–century rulers of northern Karnataka

Chennakeshava, "Beautiful Keshava"

Cholas, 9th-13th-century rulers of the Tamil country

Dasharatha, king of Ayodhya in the *Ramayana*; father of Rama

Dasoja, Hoysala artist

Dharanendra, attendant deity of Parshvanatha

Dikpalas, guardians of the eight directions of space

Draupadi, princess married to the Pandavas in the *Mahabharata*

Drona, preceptor of the Pandavas and Kauravas in the *Mahabharata*

Drupada, father of Draupadi in the *Mahabharata*

Durga, goddess who slays Mahisha

Dushasana, Kaurava warrior killed by Bhima in the *Mahabharata*

Gajalakshmi, Lakshmi being lustrated by elephants with upraised trunks

Gajendra, elephant rescued by Vishnu

Ganesha, elephant-headed son of Parvati and Shiva

Gangaraja, minister and general of Vishnuvardhana

Gangas, 8th-11th-century rulers of southern Karnataka; feudatories of the Cholas

Garuda, eagle mount of Vishnu

Ghatotkacha, warrior son of Bhima in the *Mahabharata*

gopis, herdswomen associated with Krishna

Govardhana, hill lifted by Krishna to shelter the herds of cows

Haidar Ali, ruler of Mysore, 1761-82

hamsa, goose

Hanuman, monkey general and ally of Rama in the *Ramayana*

Harihara, fused representation of Vishnu (Hari) and Shiva (Hara)

Harihara I, Vijayanagara king, ruled 1336-56

Harihara II, Vijayanagara king, ruled 1377-1404

Hidimba, demon killed by Bhima in the *Mahabharata*

Hiranyakashipu, demon king killed by Narasimha; father of Prahlada

Hiranyaksha, demon killed by Vishnu as Varaha

Hoysalas, 11th-14th-century rulers of Karnataka

Hoysaleshvara, name of the king's *linga* in the Halebidu temple

Indra, god of the heavens; one of the Dikpalas, guardian of the East

Janardhana, name of Vishnu

Jatayu, vulture who intercepts Ravana in the *Ramayana*

Jina, Jain teacher who has obtained liberation

Kailasa, mountain home of Shiva

Kakatiyas, 12th-13th-century rulers of the eastern Deccan

Kali, fierce goddess of destruction

Kaliya, serpent demon subdued by Krishna

Kalki, future *avatara* of Vishnu

Kamsa, wicked king killed by Krishna; also his uncle

Kauravas, warrior family in the *Mahabharata*, cousins of the Pandavas

Kedareshvara, name of Shiva

Keshava, name of Vishnu

Ketamalla, merchant-officer of Vishnuvardhana

Khaljis, 13th-14th-century sultans of Delhi

Kiritarjuniya, story of Arjuna winning the magic weapon from Shiva who was disguised as a hunter (*kirata*)

kirtimukha, monster face

Kirtinarayana, "Vishnu of Glory"

Krishna, hero of the *Bhagavata Purana; avatara* of Vishnu

Krishna Raja IV, Wodeyar king, ruled 1894-1940

Kurma, tortoise *avatara* of Vishnu

Lakshmana, brother of Rama in the *Ramayana*

Lakshmi, **Lakshmidevi**, consort of Vishnu

Lakshminarayana, Vishnu with Lakshmi

Lanka, island home of Ravana

linga, phallic emblem of Shiva

madanike, popular name of a bracket maiden figure

Mahabharata, epic story of the battle between the Pandavas and Kauravas

Mahisha, buffalo demon killed by Durga

makara, imaginary aquatic creature with crocodile snout

Malik Kafur, commander of the troops of the Khalji sultan of Delhi that invaded the Deccan

Mallitamma, Hoysala artist

Malwa, region of central India

Manmatha, god of love

Maricha, demon killed by Rama in the *Ramayana*

Matsya, fish *avatara* of Vishnu

Mohini, female form of Vishnu

naga, cobra

Nagareshvara, name of Shiva

naman, Vaishnava symbol

Nandi, bull mount of Shiva
Narasimha, man-lion *avatara* of Vishnu
Narasimha I, Hoysala king, ruled 1142-73
Narasimha II, Hoysala king, ruled 1220-35
Narasimha III, Hoysala king, ruled 1254-92
Narayana, name of Vishnu
Nayaka, provincial governor
Panchalingeshvara, five *linga* shrines
Pandavas, warrior family in the *Mahabharata*; cousins of the Kauravas
Pandyas, 10th-12th-century rulers of the Tamil zone
Paramaras, 10th-12th-century rulers of central India
Parashurama, *avatara* of Vishnu
Parshvanatha, 23rd Jain Tirthankara
Parvati, consort of Shiva
Prahlada, son of Hiranyakashipu; devotee of Vishnu
Putana, ogress killed by Krishna
Rama, hero of the *Ramayana; avatara* of Vishnu
Ramanuja, 11th-12th-century Shrivaishnava philosopher-teacher
Ramayana, epic story of Rama
Ranganatha, Vishnu sleeping on Ananta
Rati, consort of Manmatha
Ravana, multi-headed demon king in the *Ramayana* who abducts Sita
Sala, legendary Hoysala hero
Saptamatrikas, seven mother goddesses
Sarasvati, goddess of knowledge; consort of Brahma
Shachi, wife of Indra
Shaiva, pertaining to the cult of Shiva
shalabhanjika, maiden posed beneath a tree; maiden bracket figure
Shantaladevi, queen of Vishnuvardhana
Shantinatha, 16th Jain Tirthankara
Shiva, major Hindu cult divinity
Shrivaishnavism, Vaishnava devotional movement
Sita, wife of Rama in the *Ramayana*
Somanatha Dandanayaka, minister and commander of Narasimha III
Someshvara, Hoysala king, ruled 1235-60
Sugriva, rightful monkey king in the *Ramayana*
Surpanakha, sister of Ravana in the *Ramayana*
Surya, sun god
Tataka, demoness killed by Rama in the *Ramayana*
Tirthankara, one of a set of 24 Jain teachers
Trivikrama, giant *avatara* of Vishnu pacing out the three cosmic steps
Tughluqs, 14th-century sultans of Delhi
vahana, animal or bird mount of god or goddess
Vaishnava, pertaining to the cult of Vishnu
Vali, wrongful monkey king in the *Ramayana*
Vamana, dwarf *avatara* of Vishnu, then transformed into Trivikrama
Varaha, boar-headed *avatara* of Vishnu
Varuna, god of the ocean; one of the Dikpalas, guardian of the West
Vasudeva, father of Krishna in the *Bhagavata Purana*
Vasuki, king of the serpents
Venugopala, Krishna playing the flute
Vijayanagara, city on the Tungabhadra river; name of the 14th-16th-century kingdom of southern India

Vijayanarayana, "Vishnu of Victory"

vina, stringed instrument

Vinayaditya, Hoysala king, ruled 1047-98

Virabhadra, vengeful form of Shiva

Viranarayana, "Vishnu of Valour"

Vishnu, major Hindu cult divinity

Vishnuvardhana, Hoysala king, ruled 1108-42

Vishvakarma, legendary architect of the universe

Wodeyars, 17th-20th-century rulers of Mysuru

Yadavas, 11th-14th-century rulers of the northern Deccan

yaksha, ***yakshi***, benevolent male and female nature spirit

yali, fantastic leonine creature

Yama, god of death; one of the Dikpalas guardian of the South

Yoganarasimha, Narasimha depicted in the posture of a meditating yogi

Yoganarayana, Vishnu depicted in the posture of a meditating yogi

Yudhishthira, leader of the Pandavas in the *Mahabharata*

BIBLIOGRAPHY

Annual Reports of the Mysore Archaeological Department For the Years 1930, 1931 and *1932*, Bangalore: Government Press, 1933-35.

Coelho, William, *The Hoysala Vamsa*, Bombay: St Xavier's College, 1950.

Collyer, Kelleson, *The Hoysala Artists: Their Identity and Styles*, Mysore: Directorate of Archaeology and Museums, Government of Karnataka, 1990.

----, "Riverside Shrines of Talakad and Somnathpur", in George Michell, ed., *Eternal Kaveri: Historical Sites along South India's Greatest River*, Mumbai: Marg Publications, 1999, pp. 63-74.

Dayananda Patel, T., *The Kesava Temple at Somnathapura*, Delhi: Agam Kala Prakashan, 1990.

Dégeorge, Gerard and Amina Taha-Hussein Okada, *Hoysala: Dieux de l'Inde et Beautés Célestes*, Paris: Imprimeries Nationale, 2013.

Dehejia, Vidya and Peter Rockwell, *The Unfinished: Stone Carvers at Work on the Indian Subcontinent*, New Delhi: Roli Books, 2016, Chapter 11.

Del Bonta, Robert J., "The Hoysala Legacy", in Mulk Raj Anand, ed., *In Praise of Hoysala Art*, Bombay: Marg Publications, 1977, pp. 21-46.

----, "The Madanakais at Belur", in Joanna G. Williams, *Kaladasana: American Studies in the Art of India*, New Delhi: Oxford & IBH Publishing, 1981, pp. 27-33.

Deloche, Jean, *Military Technology in Hoysala Sculpture*, New Delhi: Sitaram Bhartia Institute of Scientific Research, 1989.

Derrett, J, Duncan, *The Hoysalas: A Medieval Indian Royal Family*, London:

Oxford University Press, 1957.

Devaraj, D.V., *History of the Somanathapura Temple-Complex (in Socio-Economic and Cultural Perspectives)*, Mysore: Directorate of Archaeology & Museums, 1994.

Dhaky, M.A., *The Indian Temple Forms in Karnata: Inscriptions and Architecture*, New Delhi: Abhinav Publications, 1977.

----, ed., *Encyclopaedia of Indian Temple Architecture, South India, Upper Dravidadesa, Later Phase, A.D. 973-1326*, New Delhi: Indira Gandhi National Centre for the Arts, 1996, Chapter 41.

Evans, Kirsti, *Epic Narratives in the Hoysala Temples: The Ramayana, Mahabharata & Bhagavata Purana in Halebid, Belur and Amritpura*, Leiden: Brill, 1997.

Foekema, Gerard, *Hoysala Architecture: Medieval Temples of Southern Karnataka Built during Hoysala Rule*, New Delhi: Books & Books, 1994.

----, *A Complete Guide to the Hoysala Temples*, Delhi: Abhinav Publications, 1996.

----, *Architecture Decorated with Architecture: Late Medieval Temples of Karnataka, 1000-1300 AD*, New Delhi: Munshiram Manoharlal, 2003.

----, *Fifteen Golden Examples: Indian Temple Architecture in Karnataka*, Bangalore: Simova, 2005.

Hardy, Adam, *Indian Temple Architecture: Form and Transformation, The Karnataka Dravida Tradition, 7th to 13th Centuries*, New Delhi: Indira Gandhi National Centre for the Arts, 1995.

Kasdorf, Katherine E., *Halebidu: A Guide to the Site and the Museum*, Bangalore: Archaeological Survey of India, 2009.

-----, *Forming Dorasamudra: Temples of the Hoysala Capital in Context*, unpublished PhD dissertation, New York: Columbia University, 2013, https://academiccommons.columbia.edu/doi/10.7916/D8VD75HC.

Krishna, M.A., *A Guide to Belur*, Bangalore: Government of Mysore, 1937.

Maity, S.K., *Masterpieces of Hoysala Art: Halebid, Belur, Somnathpur*, Bombay: Taraporevala, 1978.

Nagaraja Rao, M.S., *Kiratarjuniyam in Indian Art (With Special Reference to Karnataka)*, Delhi: Agam Kala Prakashan, 1979.

Narasimha Murthy, A.V., "A Study of the Label Inscriptions of the Hoysala Sculptors", in Frederick M. Asher and G.S. Gai, eds., *Indian Epigraphy: Its Bearing of the History of Art*, New Delhi: Oxford & IBH, 1985, pp. 215-9.

Narasimhachar, L., *A Guide to Belur*, Bangalore: Directorate of Archaeology & Museums, Government of Karnataka, 1994.

----, *A Guide to Halebid*, Bangalore: Directorate of Archaeology & Museums in Karnataka, 1994.

Narasimhachar, R., *The Kesava Temple at Somnathapur*, reprint, Mysore: Directorate of Archaeology & Museums in Karnataka, 1977.

----, *The Chennakeshava Temple at Belur*, reprint, New Delhi: Cosmo Publications, 1982.

Padmanabha, K., *Hoysala Sculptures: A Cultural Study*, Delhi: Sundeep Prakashan, 1989.

Patil, Channabasappa, *Panchatantra in Karnataka Sculptures*, Mysore: Directorate of Archaeology & Museums, 1995.

Prakash, D.S., *The Glory of the Hoysala Temples, With Special Reference to Belur, Halebid, Somanathapura and Shravanabelagola: An Introduction*, Mysuru: MaPraBha Publications, 2016.

Rajani, M.B. and K. Kasturirangam, "Multispectral Remote Sensing Data Analysis and Application for Detecting Moats Around Medieval Settlements in South India", *Journal of the Indian Society for Remote Sensing* [online, 3 January 2014].

Rekha Rao, *Apsaras in Hoysala Art: A New Dimension*, New Delhi: Aryan Books International, 2009.

Rice, Lewis B., *Epigraphia Carnatica*, Vol. V, Mangalore: Basel Mission Press, 1902.

Settar, S., *The Hoysala Temples*, 2 volumes, Bangalore: Kala Yatra Publications, 1992.

----, *Somanathapura*, Bangalore: Ruvari, 2008.

Sheik Ali, B., ed., *The Hoysala Dynasty*, Mysore: University of Mysore. 1972.

Srikantaiya, S., "The Topography of Halebid", *Quarterly Journal of the Mythic Society*, 8/3 (1918), pp. 185-204.

INDEX

Halebidu, Hoysaleshvara Temple, basement detail